DANNY'S
CHALLENGE

DANNY'S
CHALLENGE

*The true story of a father
learning to love his son*

DANNY MARDELL

Edited by Sally Weale

✳ SHORT BOOKS

First published in 2005 by
Short Books
15 Highbury Terrace
London N5 1UP

10 9 8 7 6 5 4 3

A CIP catalogue record for this book
is available from the British Library.

ISBN 1-904977-04-9

Printed in Germany
by GGP Media GmbH, Poessneck

"I would not want to go through what we've gone through again. I would never give him back, but if I had my life again..."

CHILDHOOD

Iwas born in Lauriston Road, Hackney, on November 5 1962, Guy Fawkes night. I always do things with a bit of a bang.

I was born at home, the middle son with two brothers, one a year older, one a year younger. We were Ronnie, Danny and Dave. My mum was Madeleine, my Dad was Ron, and we came from a pretty tough East End background.

We moved around a lot for a young family; we lived in Hackney, Dalston, Plaistow. Whenever the taxman knocked at the door, the old man moved. We didn't have a lot of money at that stage. It was always rented accommodation. Mum hiding from the rent man. All those old East End things.

We were never deprived of love; there was always food and we had shoes on our feet. Mum went without so we could have what we needed. There was no money for luxuries – it wasn't like it is today. These days there are opportunities and if you want to go out and earn it you can, but back then it just wasn't there to be done.

My background is East End through and through. My nan, my dad's mum, used to live in Stratford, not far from where my office is now. All the land that we're now buying up to develop, is where I used to play as a kid on a Sunday afternoon when I used to go and visit my nan. It seems weird now that we've come back to the area where my father's parents were, but quite nice to come back to your roots.

My mum's parents were from Hackney. They looked down a bit on my father's parents because back then Hackney was considered posh. My mum always said they were quite disappointed that she'd "gone down" to a Stratford boy.

They were two pretty tough East End families. On my mother's side they were hardworking – mainly in the rag trade, but my dad's family were just tough. My old man: he's hard. There's no getting away from it. Ronnie Mardell. He's a bit of a local face, I suppose you might say. He's an East End scrap metal dealer. That says it all, really, doesn't it? But he's done well out of it. He's got a beautiful penthouse overlooking the Thames. He lives the life of a playboy and he loves it. He's always at Langan's. He calls it his "café".

My grandad on my mum's side was a tailor and my nan was a presser. They all worked for the Jewish clothing factories in Brick Lane. My uncle ended up being a top presser, mum ended up being a machinist. My grandad from the other side, even when he was in his sixties, was still getting sacked from jobs for knocking out the foreman. That's the kind of guy he was, a very rough, tough man.

When my father was born, his dad had already gone to the war. He was a Desert Rat and was reported missing in action. But he wasn't missing at all. He was one of the guys who had a donkey and went forward to report on the enemy position in the desert.

Apparently, one day he spotted the Germans, and reported where they were; then he dumped the donkey, did a bunk and was listed as missing in action. The story goes he was living in Italy with some woman. No-one knew if he was alive or dead. Then, after the war, he turned up.

He was never very approachable. I don't remember ever really having a conversation with him. He was a carpenter and he used to work on the building sites where they would fire you for anything. He was one of the toughest men in the East End, and I think that's where my dad got it from.

When we were kids my old man was a bastard, and he'll admit it. I can see now he was just immature. He ended up in prison for a few years, after he got caught on an armed robbery at Ilford Films. I remember them coming around and arresting him when I was about three and four. They searched the house and found him hiding under the bed. He did his time mainly at Lowestoft and we used to go and see him every week or two.

It was very hard on my mum. She told us and everyone else that he was in hospital with a bad leg.

So when we went to see him we had to make sure we didn't sit on the bad leg. I never sussed it until I woke up in my bunk bed one day. I remember wondering why there were always these men watching us every time we went to see him, opening and locking gates.

And it suddenly clicked. It all started to fit together. He was in prison. There was nothing wrong with his leg – I was sure I'd sat on one leg one visit, and on the other leg the next time. I leant down from my bunk and asked my brother Ron. I told him I'd worked it out, that dad wasn't in hospital, he was in prison. Ron was older than me and a lot more sensible. He just said: "Don't tell mum."

We had been living in Plaistow, but when dad went to prison we moved to Southwark in south London. That was a hell of a shock. East Londoners don't normally go south. Our new home was Badminton House in Borough and they were the shittiest flats you've ever seen. It was much worse than where we'd been before. We lived there three years and I wouldn't like my kids to go through the three years we had. They were really tough. It was one of the old Peabody estates and there were some rough families living in them. It toughened us up and we became totally different kids to the ones we had been in Plaistow. I'll always remember the smell of those flats. Horrible.

Now and again I go past there, to remind myself of where I come from. It was hard, but it was the making of us as kids. Some people look at me now with my nice car and my nice suit and they think it's all been easy. Then I show them where I came from and I can see it in their faces – they're thinking, "bloody hell". And I take them round the corner to my old school, St Saviour's, with the playground on the roof. I love seeing their reaction. I like my roots. I'm very proud of where I come from.

**

Things changed when dad came home. I didn't really know him, but I learned pretty quick. There was this one particular family in Badminton House who really looked down on us. My old man had only been out on day release from prison for a couple of weeks, when there was a huge argument. It started with the kids, then this woman shouted out: "You're all fucking bastards anyway," as if we didn't have a dad, because they'd never seen our dad. Anyway, dad was there and he heard it. They didn't know what kind of dad I had. He completely lost his temper. He flew up the stairs, grabbed the father by the throat and smacked him in the head.

I remember another day this boy called John Duffy, the toughest kid in the area, beat me up. I came home from school crying. I told dad what had happened, and he asked me where John lived. I told him and we went off to find him. I remember going down the stairs thinking: "My dad's going to get John Duffy." So we found him and my dad said: "Did you beat up my son?" And John said: "Yeah." And dad said: "Right, you're going to fight him again now."

I was crying, saying I don't want to fight. But dad made us fight, and John Duffy beat me up again. Dad had a real go at me. The fact that I didn't want to fight annoyed him more than me losing the fight. He said: "You keep fighting. Don't back down to no-one." And that was the old man's attitude.

My mum was not that different. A few years later when I was at South Park Juniors in Ilford, there was a lad up the road called Wayne Hunt and he was one of the local hard nuts. He and his mates jumped me and gave me a bit of a kicking and I remember going home crying.

My dad was away at the time working in Liverpool blowing up the New Brighton pier – he was in demolition at the time. I told mum what had happened and she slapped me round the head with the dishcloth. She said: "You go up there and you bash that Wayne Hunt right now." And she threw me out of the house. She said if I didn't beat him up, she was going to whack me herself.

I was more scared of my mum than I was of Wayne so I went back up there and knocked his tooth out. And my mum was so pleased with me she made me a cake. I saw Wayne at school the next day. He was a lot tougher than me, but he wasn't going to fight me again, because he knew that I would fight back.

And that's how it is in life. If they know you're going to fight back, they'll leave you alone. Don't stand back and take it, because you'll get bullied. My parents taught me that and it hasn't stood me in bad stead since.

It was like a dream when dad finally came out of prison. All of a sudden you've got a dad! He got money again, and very quickly. I've never asked him where he got it from, but we ended up in a lovely house in Eton Road in Ilford. All of a sudden we go from this appalling block of flats to this lovely house. We're like rich kids, with these parks all around us, a garden, nice road, neighbours that aren't fighting. It was like winning the lottery. My dad was driving nice cars. We were being taken to school in a Bentley.

It was only a three-bedroom terraced house, but when we moved in it seemed like a mansion to us. They did it up like a palace. We were the first people in the road to have a colour television. My dad bought mum a fox fur, and I remember her calling it her "lonely coat" because he was never there. We were going to school in our posh leather coats. The other kids in our street were going to Pontin's and Butlin's; we were going to Rome and Spain. But it didn't last long.

Mum and dad started having some severe rows. I remember my brother and I sitting upstairs listening to what was going on. They were both pretty volatile

– it wasn't just one-sided. Then dad pissed off. He went bankrupt and we were back to nothing again. Two or three years of wealth, then it was right back to basics again. My mum always says before dad went to prison he was the hardest working family man you could come across. He was still a bit of a lad – one time he nicked the Mayor of Stratford's car to drive my Auntie Joan to her wedding – but he was a really lovely family man. Whatever prison does to a man, they don't come out the same people.

I suppose dad must have fallen in love with someone else. I can understand now that these things happen. He wanted to be with her more than he wanted to be with us. Life's too short not to be with the person you want to be with, but I do believe there's other ways of looking after your family, rather than just going off and leaving them. If you're going to do that, you need to look after your family, but he didn't.

He abandoned us. I think what he did was wrong. Now, as an adult and a father myself, I understand more why he did it. Sometimes the pressure gets on top of you and you think, "I want to go off and be by myself." I won't ever think what he did was right, but I know there's a lot of him in me.

***

My parents have been divorced 35 years or so now. It's been very bitter and has split the family for years. It's still not resolved really. I'm quite close to my dad now. He wasn't really round much when I was young. I was closer to my Uncle Brian, who was the father figure I would go and see for a chat. He was the one who first introduced me to drinking. He used to have a laugh getting me drunk on a Sunday afternoon and sending me home after three pints to my mum, who would do her nut.

As the years rolled on and I joined the forces where I really learned about serious drinking, the tables turned and it was my turn to get him drunk then send him home to his wife for a laugh. Sadly, Uncle Brian died in 2003.

My dad and I have only been really close the last two or three years. I think I needed to do quite a bit of growing up, but so did he. I was very bitter towards him. I still react even now and we have a bit of a ding-dong because of how he treated me as a kid.

When he left us, we lost our house and we had to move again, this time into Buttsbury flats in Ilford. We used to go there to ride our shiny new bikes – we knew it was where the poor kids lived. And that's where they rehoused us – I took it very badly. I felt ashamed. It was such a comedown. My mum says it changed me dramatically.

I wasn't a happy kid. I was a gobby kid and got into fights all the time. One of my earliest memories is of going to another new school, and on my very first day getting a black eye. Some kid kicked me in the eye. I punched him back and he came off worst. It was the start of a long and continuing career as a fighter.

I used to have a fight once a week, mainly with older kids. My mum used to sit me down and say: "Danny, nobody's better than you, nobody." She drummed that into me every week. And she always used to say, "Hit first, ask questions later."

It probably got me through life, but I don't agree with it. That's how I was brought up. Being a boxer now, I can understand it. He who gets the first punch in generally wins the fight. I went through life like that as a youngster. I didn't care how big they were, I just hit them and worried about it afterwards.

**

It's always the weakest we pick on, isn't it? When I was in the RAF we used to get the weakest kids, push them in a wardrobe and throw it down the stairs or through the window. I don't know how they survived. You do it because you're part of the crowd and that's what you do. If you don't, there's something wrong with you.

It was the same when I was younger. Like most children at that time, I picked on others who looked different or sounded different. I remember one particular incident in Southwark: there was a girl there with Down's Syndrome and we got to know her quite well. We made out we liked her, but really we were mocking her. She used to get what we called "the silly bus" to special school every morning with all the other kids with their tongues hanging out.

Now and again my brother Dave and I would

urinate in a bottle and pretend it was orange juice and try and make her drink it. That's what kids did, thinking it was funny. I hope she didn't drink it. Nasty horrible, ignorant kids. We thought she was something to laugh at. I remember knocking on her door one day and asking her mum if she could come out to play, and I remember her mum asking why? She knew we wanted to take the mickey out of her daughter. And the girl cried because she wanted to come out, and I remember thinking, "her mum knows that we're being nasty".

When my little Dan was first born and we found out he had Down's Syndrome, I remembered having been so horrid to that girl and I thought it was God coming back to get me. Dan's peers now will never probably be like that, which is fantastic. Increasingly, children with learning disabilities are being taught in mainstream schools, which is good not just for the child concerned, but for all the other children as well. And, in another twenty years' time, we won't see anything like the amount of prejudice against people with disabilities we still see today.

***

With all the changes we had, it was up and down like a yo yo. My mum was a good mum, she tried her best, but I just wasn't a happy kid. I got so used to fighting; I got it all worked out. My fights used to fall every Thursday – I don't know why. But I'd wear my scruffiest clothes on a Thursday, so I was ready for a scrap. But fighting didn't make me feel better. I didn't particularly enjoy it. I would rather not have had a fight, but I just wasn't going to give up. I wasn't going to back down.

Even then, I knew I was going to be a multi-millionaire. I didn't know how I was going to do it, but when I started admiring Rolls Royce cars, I knew I was going to have one. I used to watch things on television and think: "I'm going to have that, I'm going to do that, I'm going to get that."

I started working very young, from about twelve years old. I started on paper rounds, but I was very serious about it. I began with one round, but then I beat up another kid down the road and nicked his round, and quickly I built it up so I was earning quite a bit. I just wanted money in my pocket.

It was when we were moved into Buttsbury flats that I started to become obsessed with working and earning money. All of a sudden we had nothing. My mum needed help, so I got a job on a greengrocer's stall earning a fiver or a tenner a day. I started bunking off school and working instead. We were on free school meals and got free school uniforms because we were the poor kids on social security. I hated it.

I was shaped by that experience. The fact that we had money, then lost it when dad went to prison, then had it when he came out, only to lose it all over again, gave me the desire for success. I remember saying to myself: "I'm going to go and get it." And that's what I did, and that's what I have carried on doing.

As I grew older, my desire for money grew bigger. I began working for a greengrocer's on Manor Park High Road, which was right next door to the local sauna and massage parlour. The cold store for all the fruit and veg was at the back of the yard, and the girls had this little terrace and they used to sit out there topless, getting the sun on their tits. I was only twelve and they'd shout down at me: "Are you all right darling?" And I'd get all embarrassed.

And sometimes they'd come up to the stall and they'd ask for me to serve them and they'd try to embarrass me. They'd say: "I want a cucumber, Dan, a big one." And they'd giggle. I was mortified.

I used to start work before school at about six, opening up the stall. I'd leave by 8am and get the bus to school. After school I'd be there to close up shop, and I'd work all day Saturday. Sometimes I'd bunk off school altogether to work, and the last few years I was out of school more than I was in.

I was tough even back in those days. You wouldn't mess with me at school, but at that age I wasn't cool. Girls started to like me because I had a couple of quid in my pocket and I could take them out. As a schoolkid I was earning pretty good money – about £25 a week. The average earnings of a grown man weren't a lot more in those days. My mum and dad didn't have a lot of money at that time, so I started to clothe myself. My mum could afford to buy me shoes, but she couldn't afford to buy me the sort of shoes I wanted so I started becoming quite independent financially. And in the last couple of years at school I became a very cool kid.

I grew up very quickly then. I came into my own and there was a lot of respect for me. A lot of it came from the fact that I managed to beat up Nigel Benn, who was one of the toughest kids in our school. And we all know what he went on to do.

But I don't remember that period as a happy time of my life. I had some good mates and we had a laugh. I remember one time we all went down to Southend to get swallows tattooed on our hands. Just as it was my turn I backed out because I was more scared of going home to my mum with this tattoo than of my mates taking the mickey out of me. They all ended up with tattoos right up their arms. I've never had a tattoo, I've never had my ear pierced and I've never smoked. I've done everything else, but they're the three things I managed to avoid.

In my final year at school I was asked to leave because by that stage I was very disruptive and I just didn't care. I was only allowed back for English and art. I had a mate called Gavin Wilmer, and if we didn't want to do something, then we wouldn't. One time I remember he had lighter fuel which he sprayed all over our desks and we set fire to it. It was a very dysfunctional school. We didn't show any interest, so the teachers didn't show any interest in us.

The one thing I knew I wanted to do was join the RAF. As a youngster I had two fascinations. One was money and the other was planes. I had always, always loved aircraft and I wanted to become a pilot, but I didn't have the brains for it. I'd been slung out of the air cadets after getting in a fight with some skinheads from Dagenham. The squadron leader told me I wasn't the right material for an air cadet and asked me to leave. I had to give my uniform back. I still had that rebellious streak in me, so I threw it back at him, told him I couldn't care less and marched out. He told me I'd never get into the RAF in a million years, but as soon as I was old enough I went to the RAF careers office in Ilford and took the entrance exam.

I didn't do very well. They offered me a job as a dog handler, a chef, a steward or an RAF policeman. I remember sitting there and saying: "Hang on, I'm joining the RAF, I want to work on aircraft. I don't want to work with bleeding dogs." I was a right stroppy kid. But the officer told me that, given my academic performance, that was all they could offer me. He said that if I came back in six months' time and my maths was better, perhaps they could make me a better offer.

So I had to go back to school and ask for some extra help. I'd been thrown out of maths and science by my teacher, Mr Beaumont, I told him I wanted to join the RAF but my maths was not good enough. Amazingly, he agreed to help me, and at lunchtimes me and Mr Beaumont did extra maths and mechanics.

I remember all my mates taking the piss out of me, but it worked. Six months later, I took the entrance exam again and they offered me flight line mechanic, the lowest possible job you could have working on aircraft. It's the preparation of the aircraft for flight, getting the tyres ready, checking the pressure gauges, marshalling the aircraft. It was quite a simple job really, but the important thing was I was working on aircraft and I was so proud of myself. I was almost seventeen and I couldn't wait to get started.

If it weren't for the RAF I would've ended up in prison. I was heading the wrong way and the RAF straightened me out. Two of the best things I've ever done in my life was to join the RAF young and to leave it young. I came out after six years, still aged only 22, having seen a lot of the world and have enjoyed a lot of different experiences. It was a bloody good grounding.

LEAVING HOME

I've always been fascinated by aircraft. Still am really. When I was a little kid I used to make airfix planes; today if I'm at an airshow and I see a good jet flying around, I'm still interested.

As a youngster I used to have this dream of getting up there and shooting at Russians. I couldn't do that obviously, without the grades the closest thing I could do was work on the aircraft. It was one of the proudest days of my life when I got accepted in the RAF.

I had to wait a bit to join up, because I had broken my arm and they asked me to wait until it had straightened out. So I had a bit of time on my hands. I fell out with the man who owned the greengrocer's so I went down to the job centre. The first and only time I've ever done it.

There was one ad looking for a forklift truck driver: "Must be eighteen, with a full clean driving licence and able to get up early in the morning. Excellent rates of pay with plenty of overtime." I was sixteen, I didn't have a driving licence, but I could get up early in the morning, so I rang up and got an interview.

They told me I couldn't be a forklift truck driver, but they could put me on the production line. The money was good, but I was told I would have to accept less because I was only sixteen. My job was to load sacks full of pig food on to pallets ready for the fork-lift drivers. I stank. I've only ever joined a union once in my life, and it was that day.

The TGWU union rep asked if I was happy with all my terms and conditions, and I said no. "I'm not being paid as much as him over there just because I'm younger," I complained. He agreed that wasn't fair and told everyone to down tools. Half an hour later the personnel manager came out and said I was on the same pay as everyone else and I said thank you very much.

All of a sudden I'm earning bundles of money. I was taking home £60 a week and I got used to having money in my pocket. It was a horrible shock when I finally joined up – the RAF paid me £25 a week. That was never going to be enough for me. But, money apart, I really began to enjoy life. I don't think I'd ever really been happy before that.

***

My first experience of RAF life was at RAF Swinderby in Lincolnshire where I was sent for my basic training. I remember my mum and my brother Ron came to Ilford station to see me off. My mum was crying. I paid 5p for a platform ticket for her to see me off, but I wouldn't pay for my brother, so we had an argument. My mum's crying because I've joined up and I'm leaving home, and her two sons are kicking the hell out of each other over a 5p platform ticket. Stupid.

When the train pulled away, I remember thinking:

"Bloody hell, what have I gone and done here?"

I got on the train at King's Cross and there were loads of blokes just like me, fresh-faced lads, barely shaving, all looking around at each other on the train, not sure who to talk to. Somehow we all ended up talking and by the end of the journey, we're all excited, we're ready, like a unit, together, right from the beginning.

My first memories of Swinderby were the drill officers, their caps pulled down to their noses, shouting and bullying us. We'd only just stepped off the train and there they were ordering us around, abusing us, shoving us onto the most uncomfortable bus in the world. After the camerarderie of the train ride we all fell silent.

So this was it. Six months of yelling and square bashing as they struggled to mould us into servicemen who would do as they were told.

The first three days were awful. It was bloody freezing. I was a boy from London. I wasn't used to the bleak Lincolnshire weather, the open fields and the wind howling through from the Wash. They got us up at ungodly hours, marching into our dormitory at five in the morning, clashing metal bins, making a terrible noise.

I was in a dormitory of about twenty-four blokes and all you've got is a bed and a locker. It was such a shock. After three days I'd had enough. I wanted to go home. I rang my mum and told her I didn't like it. She was crying on the phone, but she told me I wasn't coming home. She told me to stick it out. My uncle Brian had once joined the merchant navy and he'd done exactly the same as me. After three days he rang his mum and begged to come home. She told him to pack his bags and he'd regretted it ever since. She's a strong woman, my mum.

That night, after talking to mum, I went down the Naafi and began to get to know the other lads. We went out drinking and we got totally slaughtered, which was completely against the rules but we had a right bloody laugh. The next day I got up and I thought: "This is good. I'm enjoying this. I haven't got my mum telling me off. I can get home when I like. Yeah, I'm going to stick with this." And that was the turning point.

Within a couple of weeks, we were getting the

whole thing sussed. You form your little cliques and you work out who's good at what. My skill was creases in trousers. My grandad was a tailor and he'd shown me how to use tailor's soap, which gave you the most beautiful creases. The other lads didn't know anything about my tailor's soap – all they knew was I was great at pressing trousers. I did all the trousers; they did my boots and bedpack ready for inspection every morning.

We all had our jobs and we worked together. That's what the forces are trying to make you do so, come a situation where someone's shooting at you, you've got someone who's good at firing, someone who's good at loading and you're part of a team.

They nicknamed me "Cockney", because I was the only gobby Londoner there. I grew up a lot in those weeks. We had our passing out day and I remember being so proud, standing there in my number one uniform, marching in front of my mum and my brother Ron. In those six weeks they'd taught me how to march, how to throw a rifle round; they'd got me fit and made me part of a team. We'd seen a lot of lads leave because they couldn't handle it; they went off with their kit bags and they were like dead men walking. You didn't feel sorry for them. You felt: "Well, you're not right for us." Whether they gave up on the RAF or the RAF gave up on them, we didn't want them around.

**

It was in the RAF that I really developed an interest in boxing. I'd started doing a bit in my last year at school. I was a scrapper in those days. I wasn't a boxer at all. I'd done a bit of training, though, and one day this bloke called Lloyd Day – who was as tough as old boots – asked me if I wanted to have a sparring session with him. I told him I didn't know how to spar so he said: "Just put the gloves on, I'll come at you, and you just try your best."

My technique as a fighter had always been to start with a kick in the nuts, so that's exactly what I did that first time in the ring. I saw this big tough bugger coming for me and my first reaction was to kick him straight in the nuts. It was instinct – I was going to survive the only way I knew how. Lloyd was very calm about it. He said: "No Dan. You don't do it like that." And bang, bang, bang, he knocks me all over the place, and shows me what it's all about. And that was my first introduction to boxing.

I didn't do much at that stage. I just went and trained a few times, but already I knew I liked it. My mum hadn't wanted me to box. She thought it was too dangerous. But she'd said if I wanted to do it when I was older, I could. So that's what I did. I waited.

After Swinderby, I was sent to RAF Halton, near Aylesbury, to learn my trade as a flightline mechanic, but it was at Halton that I developed my passion for boxing. They had a good boxing club there and one night a couple of weeks after arriving I went with my mate Geordie to see a boxing match – the RAF v the Army. Delroy Parks, who went on to become a very good professional boxer was fighting for the RAF – I watched this and thought, "right, I'm going to do it". So Geordie and I started training with a guy called Roy Rigg who was in charge of RAF boxing training. I spent about three months at Halton doing my basic flightline mechanic training. It was an eventful time for me – I lost my virginity there. I wonder what happened to her? And at the end of it, there were a number of postings available.

My main ambition was to get abroad, so I selected postings with aircraft that I thought would be involved in overseas missions. I put my name down for 55 and 57 squadron, based near King's Lynn in Norfolk, working on Victor tankers. The Victor is an inflight refueller and my theory was that wherever a squadron goes in the world, you've got to take a Victor and its ground crew too, so the chances were there would be plenty of travel.

I spent five years at RAF Marham about twelve miles outside King's Lynn. It's the most desolate place. I remember being on the train and as we got closer it got bleaker and bleaker. It's just fields. I was still only seventeen and it looked horrible. That's where I started my real boxing. But it didn't start well. I'd only been there a week when I got into trouble. I was there sitting on a table when one of the older lads came in and told me to get off the table. I didn't like the way he talked to me so I told him to take a running jump. He whacked me and I completely lost it. I chased him up the corridor and smacked him really hard. I left him on the floor and went off to the gym to start boxing.

The RAF police arrived. I was arrested and charged with assault. I was fined £25 and got my "jankers", which is like loss of privileges. I didn't think anything of it at the time, but that's why my career in the RAF never went anywhere. If I'd been in the marines or paras they'd have accepted it was a fight, but in the RAF they don't like fighters.

**

I joined the boxing club which was run by a lovely guy called Flight Lt Brian Chillery. I was the first to join; others followed and we began to build up the bones of a boxing team at RAF Marham. After about eight months' training, Mr Chillery entered me into the Wakefield Championships, which is held at RAF St Athan in Wales for RAF novices who've been in "Under-ten" fights.

We all went from Marham – me, Gary Ellinger, Ginger, Frankie Gentles. There were hundreds of novices gathering to fight each other and find out who was going on to represent the RAF. I was eleven stone two, a six-foot beanpole with fantastic reach, and I'd never been in the ring. The championships were being staged in this hangar where there were three rings and fights going on all day. I had one fight in the morning and beat this bloke quite convincingly on points. In the afternoon I was in the ring again, and I knocked this bloke all over the place. They had to stop the fight after the first round. I remember thinking: "God almighty, I'm good." I rang my mum and Ron that night, and it was fantastic, I felt really proud of myself.

The next morning, they put me in another fight. I'm so confident I feel like I'm the next Wakefield champion. My next fight, I'm knocking the granny out of this bloke from Brize Norton but at the end they gave the decision to this other bloke. And I'm standing there – robbed.

I went away from RAF St Athan not very happy. But that's just the way boxing goes. The rest of my mates did pretty well, and all in all the "Marham Marauders", as we had become known, were starting to get a good reputation for themselves.

***

The next big championship was the RAF "Under-19s" tournament at RAF Lyneham. Again I had two fights – I knocked both my opponents out in the first round and the second fella was an RAF policeman, which was particularly pleasing. I got to the final and I felt like I was going to win the championship. That's how I used to go to every fight. But the bloke I fought made an absolute fool of me. He played to the crowd; he boxed me all over the place because I didn't have the experience. I'd been in about five fights, he'd been in a hundred and fifty. But I knew I was tougher than him and I felt like he'd stolen my championships. I went to his changing room afterwards and beat him up. It wasn't a very good thing to do, I know, but that's what I did.

The next thing I know is Roy Rigg has put me in the RAF "Under 19s" team. We spent two weeks training at Ruddlow Manor, the underground listening base in Wiltshire, but by this time I'm beginning to get interested in women. The first night we were there we went to a local nightclub and started chatting up a couple of girls. One of them, it turns out, was Roy's daughter, Sue – a very pretty girl.

You know how they talk about women ruining your boxing? Well Sue ruined mine. I was meant to be in intensive training, but in fact I was having a laugh with the boxing trainer's daughter. All the rest periods I was meant to be having, I was sneaking off with Sue. The next fight was at RAF Hullavington, which is a para base in Oxfordshire, and we were up against Oxford University.

I go to this fight, but I've been up all night with Sue and I've had no bloody rest. This university chap walks in; he's good-looking and flash. He's got a woman on each arm and I'm thinking: "I'm gonna kill you, you flash git." I thought I'd beat him easily because I was a tough East End lad, and he was just a university boy. I didn't realise that you could be clever and hard at the same time, but he was really hard. He bashed me all round the ring. I think it was Sue's fault. I was just tired out.

***

By this time I had started drinking a bit as well, which I'd never done before. I thought that I could train five days a week, get drunk on Friday and Saturday, and go back on Monday for training and a fight. But it quickly became clear that I couldn't.

One Monday morning, I'd been pissed all weekend, and Chillery came into my room and said: "Dan I want you to fight tonight against the Friar's boxing club in King's Lynn. Be ready at 6pm."

King's Lynn at that time was the home of a gang called the Wildcats. They knew me because I'd already had a number of run-ins with them. That night I was the only RAF man at the club. They put me in the last fight of the night, against the star of the show, a bloke who was two weights up on me. They just wanted a good show – I'd done a full day's work, I'd been pissed all weekend, and I was knackered.

He got in the ring and he was as tough as nails. He was covered in tattoos, his muscles are bulging and he was glaring at me, this skinny kid from the forces. About forty seconds into the fight, he came steaming in; I covered up and I nutted him. I didn't mean to, but the top of my head went right across his eye and his eye opened up. Then I hit him bam on the eye again and I completely mullahed his eye. The crowd went bananas. They gave me the fight and I got out of there pretty quick.

They're starting to call me the "Star of Marham". Brian Chillery finds me another fight on the Wednesday night against a policeman. I was feeling quite confident by then. I'd had six or seven fights, and I thought I wasn't a bad fighter. This copper had had about fifty fights, but he hadn't been in the ring for a year. I absolutely killed him in the first round. They stopped the contest and gave me the fight. I'd walked away with two beautiful trophies within three days.

At that point I heard from Roy Rigg who invited me to fight in the combined services "Under 19s". It's very prestigious – the army, RAF and navy all battle it out to find out who's the best. And from that you normally go on to ABA titles, which are the pinnacle of amateur boxing. Most of our world champions have been ABA finalists.

***

So my boxing career was going well but, just as that door opened, my RAF career also took off. I turned eighteen and at eighteen they let you fly abroad. That had always been one of my chief motivations for joining the services, so instead of pursuing the boxing, I took up the offer of a two-week stint at an airforce base in Nebraska which was hosting a bombing competition. I regret it now, but I said no to combined services and went instead to America. That was the closest I ever came to breaking into serious boxing. If I hadn't gone to America I might have made it.

By this stage I was starting to drink quite seriously. Squadron life is all about drinking. It's one big piss-up, and it was starting to affect my boxing. I was still having the odd fight, but I wasn't putting into it like I had done before. I stopped for a little while and started going out with this girl, but then I got into this big punch-up. It was the Friday night bop and they brought in all the King's Lynn girls and it was rough. Before I got down to the disco that night, there'd been a horrendous punch up – one bloke had glassed another. Three RAF policemen were there trying to keep order.

I'm not saying I was a hard fella, but I was a boxer. I was fit and I could fight so I went in there, beat the hell out of five blokes and then walked out, not thinking about the consequences. It was a really big fight. There was tension building up on the base and the RAF had to restore order fairly quickly, so they had to find someone to make an example of. Who better then me? That big-headed, mouthy boxer Danny Mardell.

They sent in the Special Investigation Branch and that's when you know you're in the shit. When they can't deal with it on base, they call in the SIB from off base. Like an idiot I owned up to everything I'd done.

They couldn't have had an easier nick. The RAF police wanted me court-martialled for five counts of assault, which would have meant six months, military prison and then I would have been slung out of the airforce. It was starting to dawn on me how serious this was. But the group captain in charge of the station was a big boxing fan and I was his pride and joy. I was a star, I was knocking out people and he liked it.

So a deal was brokered. Rather than a full trial, I accepted the station officer's discretion, which gave me twenty-eight days in prison in Colchester, then a return to the RAF. I couldn't believe it. Here I was in the forces, I'd had a fight and I was being sent to prison!

I was hauled in front of the station commander, pleaded guilty and accepted my punishment. Twenty-eight days might not sound long but they made it as nasty as they could. I was put away over Christmas. To be honest, I was shitting myself. I'd heard some horrendous stories about Colchester and how tough it was. The snow was very heavy that Christmas so they put me in the cells in the guard room that night and took me the next day to Colchester in a Vauxhall Chevette.

As we were driving, the snow became heavier and heavier. I was hoping we'd have to run back, but we made it. I was put in a Nissan hut with about sixteen blokes and one stove. It was freezing cold.

The other fellas, it all turned out, came from the marines. And they were bloody great. I got a bit of stick because I was a blue job – ie RAF – but I was as fit as they were if not fitter, so I got a lot of respect for that. They were also impressed that I was in on five counts of assault. I had to be a geezer!

The biggest currency in there was cigarettes. I've never smoked, so I bought loads of cigarettes and secretly held them back. One week later when they'd all run out of cigarettes, out came my fags and I started making deals. Bed packs, boots, extra food – and I'm sitting there like bloody Lord Muck negotiating deals for cigarettes. The entrepreneur came out in me and within a few days I'd got everybody running around for me. And to cap it all they let me out after twenty-four days for good behaviour.

I came out just after New Year. I went back to my base and within a few days the RAF called me and asked me to box for them. I said: "No, I'm not boxing for you. You've just put me away for fighting, I'm in a fighting force, I've had a punch up – and you put me away and you wanted to sling me out. I won't fight for you." As soon as I refused to fight, my career went tumbling down very quickly.

I boxed at the King's Lynn gym for a while, but by this time I was going out with this girl Lynne Wright. I was going out at weekends and my last fight I got beaten quite convincingly. You can't hide in a ring. If you're not putting the work in, you're not going to see a result at the end of it. That's what happened to my boxing career. It was cut short at nineteen years old. A lot of it was my fault, but with the right guidance I could have gone a lot further.

***

Once the boxing stopped I had a great time travelling in the RAF. I went to Bermuda, Nebraska, Azores, Ascension Island, Africa, Banjal and Cyprus. They were only short trips – a couple of weeks. The Bermuda trip was only meant to be four days but we kept breaking our aircraft on purpose. We took five aircraft out there and every one of the planes was needed. If one part broke, the whole ground crew had to stay. Every day we broke one part of an aircraft. This must have cost hundreds of thousands of pounds to the taxpayer. They had to get the Hercules to fly back to England, get the part and fly back again. The next day we'd break another part, just to stay out there.

In the end the RAF went very wrong for me. I was

charged twenty-three times, mainly for fighting and insubordination. I became a bit of a pain in the neck. I was very anti-establishment, a bit of a rebel. If there was a way around it, I'd find it and I was a bit of a bad influence on the lads in the squadron. If it was happening, I was involved in it. I was coming home weekends to London and that's when I began to realise I had to make money.

One of the fashions in London at that time was leather string vests made in Turkey. I bought a thousand of them and I took them up to King's Lynn, put a huge mark up on them and sold them to all the stalls and shops. My room was like Arthur Daley's office. I had things piled up before taking them out to sell.

Then I bought a load of kids' clothes – nine Geest banana boxes full – for £50. I walked round the married quarters next day knocking on all the doors, selling kid's clothes. I was very successful, I made a lot of money. I began thinking: "How can I expand this, get some real business going?"

My next plan was a river trip down the Thames. I sold loads of tickets around King's Lynn, but the weekend of the outing the Port of London river authority went on strike and the whole thing had to be called off. Everyone was after me trying to get their money back, but I'd already spent it.

At this stage I was nearly twenty-two. I knew I didn't want to be in the airforce, but I had eighteen months left. I was nothing but a pain in the neck to the RAF by this time. They finally agreed to give me an administrative discharge. It's when the RAF and the individual agree to go different ways. It's hard to get one. If you want to get out, normally you have to pay, buy your way out. And I got out for nothing.

When they finally confirmed I was out, that was when I really started to worry. Things had been safe in the force – suddenly I was being let loose on the world. What would it be like? I tell you, it was fantastic. I'd managed to blag my way into a job in Saudi Arabia, working for the American firm Lockheed Arab, on Hercules aircraft. I knew nothing about Hercules aircraft, but I got the job.

***

The job wasn't quite what I thought it was. I thought

I was going there to do airframes, that was my job, an airframe engineer. But when I got out there I found I was called the crew chief. A crew chief in the American airforce is responsible for the whole bleeding aircraft. The airframes, engines, electrics, you have to get the lot ready. So I'd got the responsibility now to sign for the aircraft, that it was safe to fly! And I knew nothing.

As luck would have it, when I got to Saudi, they put me in this apartment where all the Lockheed guys lived in Riyadh. It was run by ninety per cent Americans. The first apartment they put me into, there was this guy called Bobby Robinson and he was an American who'd been in Saudi for about fifteen years, and he was just completely in love with aircraft, and knew them like the back of his hand.

I was told it would take three weeks to get my pass ready before I could go and work on the base. So I actually confessed to Bobby after a couple of days that I knew absolutely nothing about the aircraft. He couldn't believe it, but he helped me. He got together all the manuals and using the textbooks he showed me exactly what I needed to know.

They gave me a trainee who was a Saudi air force warrant officer to work with. I've got Philippinos working for me, I've got Pakistanis working for me; I've got my own crew. I'm twenty-two and I'm running the bloody thing. I didn't know what was happening. I just had to bullshit my way through. But I got through it, and I got through it so well that I got a commendation and was put on King Fahad's flight.

***

The big problem with Saudi is you can't drink. Absolutely not. After a very short time I became aware that almost everyone was brewing their own booze. You're not allowed to drink, but if you brew your own booze, drink it on your complex and you're sensible, and you don't go outside and get drunk, you can get away with it. So I started to learn how to brew my own stuff – we had Jeddah gin and Riyadh red. And after a couple of months I found my own set of friends and we all moved into a different apartment together in this complex.

I started to get a bit wise to the system. These Hercules aircraft are flying out of Saudi airspace everyday, sometimes to Manchester, sometimes to Dubai. I started getting a bit friendly with the pilots and flight engineers and paid them to bring in some proper booze. Now I'm making bundles of money. Not only am I earning good money in my job – £25,000 a year tax-free – I'm making a fortune out of the booze.

Saudi was full of young nurses and they all started to hear about this geezer Danny Mardell who was a fitness fanatic, who had his own bar in his apartment, and had access to any alcohol they might fancy. I was coining it, and I was having the wildest parties Saudi Arabia's ever seen. I used to work the graveyard shift, 12 midnight until 7am. Nothing flew so I would get my head down for three or four hours, run back to the apartment, swim fifty lengths, then all the nurses would turn up after their night shift. We'd close all the curtains, crank the music up, put on sunglasses and have a party. It was fantastic. I fell in love out there for the first time in my life. She was called Gill.

***

We had some real fun, but it was too good to last. I was making too much dough. Lockheed tried to calm me down by changing my shifts, but eventually I got the sack. I was actually escorted out of the country. I've got to tell you, I cried, I physically cried. When they put me in that cab to take me to the airport – Gill came to say goodbye – it was terrible. The emotion just welled up and I cried my bleeding eyes out. I didn't want to lose that country.

If I could have one year of my life over again it would be that one. In Saudi. I know it sounds terrible, what with my children and my family, but oh, send me back to Saudi. It was great. For the first time in my life I had money in my pocket, real money without worries. I didn't have to worry about some airforce dickhead telling me what to do; I had independence; I had a job I was enjoying; I had the heat and I was flying to Bangkok every few weeks. I was twenty-two years old and I was living the life of Riley.

BREAKING THE RULES

I came back to the UK from Saudi in 1985 and had to start from scratch really. I'd earned a lot of money out there, but I'd spent most of it. The rest was lost in a poor investment.

I started going out with an old girlfriend of mine called Keely. We'd been in touch for many years. I'd first met her at Barking Park when I was thirteen and she was about ten or eleven.

She was one of these girls who seemed untouchable to me. I just loved her the day I met her, and all I'd ever do was take her out and give her the odd kiss good night. I put her on this pedestal. I wrote to her for years, and when I was in the forces I used to come home and see her at weekends.

When I came back from Saudi, her sister was getting married and they invited me to the wedding. Something just clicked. She was with her boyfriend, but somehow she was looking at me in a quite different way and it was obvious we should get together. I started taking her out and within a few weeks she'd agreed to marry me. I was probably on the rebound a bit after Gill in Saudi, but I didn't believe it at the time. We must have been bang in love, me and Gill, though I didn't realise. Even though Gill was married, when she heard I was getting married to Keely she flew back to try to persuade me I was making a mistake. We had a fantastic night together, but when Gill went back to Saudi I decided to go ahead with the wedding.

***

I got a job in sales and after a few interviews ended up selling showers. They had these demonstrators who worked in supermarkets; they'd tell people all about these fantastic showers and would arrange a visit. My job was to go round to their house, carry out a survey and sell them a shower. I did very well. Selling to people in their homes is not easy, but I sold a lot of showers and made a lot of money very quickly. I obviously had a knack for it.

Keely and I got married in a church in Dagenham. The reception was in the social hall next door. It was a proper white wedding with a Rolls Royce and a free bar. To be honest, the day we got married I realised I shouldn't be doing it. I thought it might get better. I loved her, but I wasn't *in* love. We spent the first week of married life in her sister's house in Tilbury because we had nowhere to live. Keely was still working at her dad's delicatessen stall in Hampstead. I was selling the showers, but I'd started looking for a different job. I noticed an advertisement offering work in the City earning thousands of pounds a week. I liked the sound of that, so I rang up.

The job was selling typewriters, which sounded OK. But what was really brilliant was the three-week intensive sales training – you had to pass the course before they offered you a job. As soon as I saw City

Business Machines, I knew it was right for me. It was very regimented, very much like the forces. All the young salesmen were wearing sharp blue suits, white shirts, blue ties and highly polished shoes. I went along to a couple of the firm's offices, and sitting outside there were Porsches, BMWs and Ferraris. All out of selling typewriters. They were earning big bucks. This was in the mid-Eighties when everybody had loads of money. And I sat down and thought, I can do this.

The course was tough – a twelve-hour day, with just a half-hour break, but they taught me everything. It was all about sales techniques, teaching you how to open, close, handle rejections, body language. It was fantastic. I really enjoyed it. It was high pressure, but it was such a laugh. And, as the days and weeks rolled on, more and more blokes dropped out. Just like the forces again. It was the survival of the fittest.

They taught us how to be professional salesmen. I came away from that course feeling that being a salesman is nothing to be ashamed of. I'm a professional. I know how to sell and that course was one of the best things I've ever done. I remember the day that I was finishing the course. They stood everybody up and told us whether we'd passed or not. The chief instructor got to me and said: "I don't think your accent's quite right for the City, but I think you're going to be the most fantastic salesman. Welcome aboard." It was a brilliant feeling. I walked out thinking, I'm going to do really well here. I began at a branch in Bethnal Green and my job was to walk round the City with these big bloody typewriters, knocking on doors, trying to get these machines placed on trial.

The aim was to get two typewriters on trial each day – one in the morning and one in the afternoon, by hook or by crook. By the end of the week if you'd got 10 typewriters on trial you might sell one or two of them. If you sold four or five typewriters a month, you'd earn a bundle of money because they were very expensive. Within a few weeks, I was doing all right. In the first six months we weren't entitled to much commission – most of it went to the sales manager and group manager. With the group manager, if the whole team doesn't reach target, he doesn't get paid very well. I didn't think it was fair that he was getting commission for sales that I secured, so I got all these deals together behind everyone's back and told him I wouldn't put them through the company unless he gave me some of his bonus. He could see the sense of what I was saying.

I broke a lot of rules back then. I started selling off the returned trial typewriters and not putting them through the company, which was a bit cheeky. But within about four or five months I was taking home about £1500 a week, which was good money in 1985. It was a bit like dog eat dog. If anybody tried to rip me off, I became quite aggressive. It's a terrible thing to say, but I got this air of menace into that company. People knew that if they did a deal with me they had to be careful. By the end of it, I had this underground business within the business, and that's how I was starting to make the dough. Maybe it was just the old East End side of me coming out. We were fairly dishonest young men at the time and we were just trying to make as much money as we could. I've never stuck to the rules and that's how I've ended up taking a lot of money.

I spent about nine months at that company. Then I won the biggest deal I'd ever had – an order for £80,000 worth of stuff – of which £20,000 was profit – from the Prudential. It wasn't a deal I could really nick or do anything with, so I took it back to the company, but the day I walked in with the order, there was obviously something major going on. Everyone was busy and I didn't have a chance to tell anyone so I put it in my pocket.

That night they got us all together and told us we were going into receivership. There was terrible doom and gloom. But there I am sitting on an £80,000 order that no-one knows about! In the end I took the deal to another company, OSS, which was run by an old mate of mine, and with it secured a partnership. I'd gone from being a trainee salesman one day, to being a partner the next!

We started off selling typewriters, but a clever engineer called Kevin Shacklock, whom we hired to service the machines, convinced us that copiers were where the big money was. Thank you Kevin! We secured a dealership with Ricoh, a huge global company which had only recently moved into the UK. They gave us a £20,000 unsecured credit limit straightaway, and a £20,000 target that had to be achieved in six months. As luck would have it, I sold £20,000 worth of copiers in just one week.

As a reward Ricoh took me to Jamaica on an all-expenses trip with all the top dealers in the UK. It was a big turning point in my life. I met some very, very wealthy men, who had made a fortune out of photocopiers. For the first time I realised I had the potential to make millions.

Back home we started building a fairly successful business, but I wanted more. My partner was more of a steady Eddie than me. He wasn't prepared to take the risks that I was, so we had a few fallings out. I finally decided I wanted out. I bought him out and went alone, renaming the company BOSS, and I carried on, owning the whole company, selling copiers and fax machines. Within a few months I was starting to make a couple of quid and it was beginning to go to my head. I began to think of myself as the successful businessman; I was taking money out of the company as I saw fit, and splashing out on my first flash car, a seven series BMW.

At that time Keely and I were living in a rented flat, but after about a year I bought a place in Seymour Gardens, Ilford. I paid £52,000 for a one-bedroom flat in a converted house. It was a lovely little place; Keely loved it. She thought we were love's young dream, but it was becoming increasingly apparent to me that my marriage was doomed. Basically, I fancied other girls and I didn't want to settle down, so I started seeing other women. Poor Keely didn't have a clue.

After Seymour Gardens, I bought a three-bedroom house in Abbey Lane in Stratford. Keely nearly died when I told her. I didn't even consult her. I just told her we were selling the flat, and moving to the house which I was going to convert into two flats. She really didn't want to move. But she went along with me. Next I bought another house, this time in Thurleston Avenue in the posh end of Ilford. It was like a dream for me. As a boy I used to walk around that area, looking at the rich kids. But then, within a few months, the property market crashed. I'd got two houses worth £50,000 less than the price I paid for them.

Then I got the worst possible news I could imagine. Keely told me she thought she was pregnant. That's when I realised I definitely did not want to be in this marriage. I didn't want to have a baby, and I definitely didn't want to have one with Keely. That afternoon when she told me, we went round her mum's house for dinner and everybody was congratulating us, but I told them I didn't want a baby. You could have cut the atmosphere with a knife.

To this day I don't know exactly what happened, but a few days later Keely told me she didn't think she was pregnant after all. There weren't that many tears. I never really got to the bottom of it, but a few weeks later I sat her down and told her everything I had been up to over the past months – the women, the affairs, the lies. I knew it would be the end of the marriage. She left me and went to her mum's. It was sad, but I'm glad I did it then rather than later when there might have been children around to hurt.

***

After that I really started enjoying myself. I was now

putting quite a bit of money in my own pocket and I was out most nights in the West End, in a flash chauffeur-driven car. I was going to nightclubs and getting my name about.

One of my favourite haunts was a place in Stratford called the Phoenix Apollo. It was the trendy place to go back then. All your "Page 3" girls went there; all the footballers; Nigel Benn always had his fight parties there; when Terry Marsh got the "Not guilty" for shooting Frank Warren, everyone went back there. It was the East End place to be seen.

I was a bit of a regular in the Phoenix Apollo. I had a £2,000 credit limit and whenever I walked in, I'd order champagne. I was a bit of a dickhead looking back. One night my mate Kelvin and I were having a drink in our local, the Wheelers, before going to a party for the West Ham football team at the Phoenix. In walks this vision.

It was Carol. She's a good-looking woman now, but at 22 with her skirt half way up her backside she was stunning. I said: "Jesus, look at her." There was only one place she was going dressed the way she was – the Phoenix. I told Kelvin I was going to pull her. He said:

"You won't." Later at the Phoenix, there she was. I went up and started chatting to her, and then this voice said: "Do you want a drink or not?" It was a really hard voice. It was her boyfriend. He didn't like me talking to her. We exchanged a few words, then left it at that. I walked off thinking, "That's a bloody shame".

I also had a girlfriend at this time – a hairdresser from Tottenham – but I couldn't get Carol out of my mind. I started going down the Wheelers just in case I bumped into her. I did. I told her I'd like to see her again and asked her for her phone number but she wouldn't give it. She did take mine, though, and a few days later I got a phone call from her mate, tipping me off that Carol was down the Wheelers if I was interested.

I dropped everything and just shot down there. To this day Carol denies she had anything to do with that phone call. Who cares. I found her. I fell in love with her. In fact I think I fell in love with her the day I set eyes on her.

DANNY IS BORN

We got married on a beach in Mauritius. Carol was twenty-four, I was thirty and we had a wonderful three-week holiday. The wedding itself wasn't that memorable. It was nice enough, but there was only me and Carol there. The reason we got married abroad was because there were disputes within our families – this person wasn't talking to that person. It was all very complicated, so we thought it wasn't worth all the trouble of involving the family, and decided to do it on our own abroad. Well, I decided it really. Carol had reservations, but at the time I didn't realise how unhappy about it she was. She went along with it.

Nevertheless, we had a lovely time. When we got back, Carol went back to her job in the buying department at C&A in Marble Arch. I still had the two houses in Ilford and Stratford, but the property market had crashed. I'd bought each of them for about £95,000. At that point they were each worth £75,000. They were going down and down in value and the interest rates were going up. Luckily I was earning enough money to be able to afford the mortgages. Everyone else was just giving their keys back to their mortgage companies, so I decided to do the same and plead poverty. They weren't keen on taking the properties back but I'd decided I wanted to buy a bigger place instead. They caught up with me in the end and I had to pay them back what I owed, but it served its purpose at the time.

I'd found this beautiful house in Wanstead. There are two particularly prestigious roads in Wanstead, one called The Avenue and one called Grove Park. When I was in the RAF I went out with this girl who lived in The Avenue in this beautiful big house. I went to pick her up one day in my Mark 3 Cortina for which I'd paid £15 and her dad blanked me. I remember pulling up and he said to her right in front of me: "I don't want you to see him again." I obviously wasn't good enough to go out with his daughter. That stuck in my mind and I thought "Sod you!" And I decided I was going to buy a house in The Avenue and I was going to show that bastard.

And years later I did! Not in The Avenue, but Grove Park, which was just as good. Number 39, Grove Park. It was in a derelict state when we bought it. The estate agent wanted £185,000, but I managed to get them down to £125,000 in the end. I'd got a bargain. Now it's worth £800,000. It felt really good. It was right round the corner from that bastard who thought I wasn't good enough for his daughter, and my house was bigger than his house. It sounds pathetic now, but it meant a lot to me.

***

Things started to go very well for me. As soon as I got the house in Wanstead, everything really took off.

That's what started Boss Property. I was looking for a property for my business and I heard about this place in Sugarhouse Lane in Stratford. They wanted £550,000 for the site. The company in there, Albany Packaging, had gone bust and the liquidator, Arthur Andersen in Manchester, wanted a fairly quick sale. I told them I could complete in a week and, after a bit of wheeling and dealing, I bought it for £320,000.

Carol was on the pill at that time. We spoke about having a family, but we weren't desperate. All I was thinking about back then was the business, but Carol came off the pill and very soon she was pregnant. We hadn't been desperate to have children, but when it happened we were very happy to be having a baby.

We found out who the best doctor was in our area – a consultant called Mr Annan and we paid to see him privately. I remember that, as part of one of our routine consultations, he told us about Down's Syndrome and suggested we went to King's College Hospital in Dulwich to have something called a mucal fold test. He told us how the test worked, and said he thought all expectant mothers should have one. It was far less invasive than amniocentesis, and involved a scan of the baby to measure the back of its neck. The measurement gives an indication of the risk of the child being born with Down's Syndrome.

The test was carried out by Professor Kypros Nicolaides who pioneered this test. We weren't in the least bit worried about it. Carol wasn't particularly old to be having her first child. We did it because we were advised to; we didn't really think about it, and the result was good news. We were told we were in the lowest possible risk category – that the risk of us having a child with Down's was 1 in 800.

We had already decided that if there was a possibility of having a baby with Down's we would have a termination. We'd talked about it and that was our position. I hadn't really been exposed to people with Down's to know much about it, but I just knew that I wasn't going to have a Down's kid myself. That was my attitude. I didn't want a kid with a learning disability. Carol probably didn't feel it as strongly as I did, but she agreed.

So off we went, thinking there was no problem at all. Everything seemed to be going really well. Then, about a week before Dan was born, I was having lunch with my mate Peter de Costa in the West End when Carol rang me up and said she was having a few stomach pains. She went to the doctor and he rushed her into Whipps Cross Hospital. They were worried that the baby was in distress because his heart rate was irregular. Sometimes it was normal, then it would plunge right down. They found he was strangling himself with the umbilical cord. They were considering there and then whether to give her an emergency Caesarean.

They baby was monitered for about 24 hours and things seemed to settle down, so they decided to leave it and let us go home. We went to see Mr Annan again, and he said he thought Carol ought to go back into hospital. They rushed her in again on February 13 1995. We were there all day and all night, as they monitored the baby's heartbeat and Carol. Then early in the morning, all of a sudden, they made a decision. I'd never seen anyone or anything move so quickly. One minute they were just monitoring Carol and the baby, the next there was this terrifying rush. They came in and said: "Sign this." They thought the baby was in trouble, that they had to get him out straight away.

They put an epidural in Carol's spine and rushed her straight in to the theatre.

It was awful. Carol was crying her eyes out. There she was telling me she loved me, I was telling her I loved her. We were looking at each other. Oh it was horrible. I thought I was going to lose her. As they took her off for an emergency Caesarean I tried to follow her but they stopped me. It was about two or three in the morning. I walked out of the maternity ward into the car park scared out of my wits. I knew Carol was in trouble. I wasn't that worried about the baby, I hadn't really identified with the baby at all. I was just concerned about Carol. I sat outside crying my bloody eyes out, not knowing what was going on.

I went back in and about three quarters of an hour later they emerged from the operating theatre. We had a little boy, they said. And there he was. They'd washed him down and he was wrapped up into a little bundle. He was only tiny – about 5lbs when he was born. Our baby.

TERRIBLE TIMES

So there I was – with my son. It was the most emotional time. He was so beautiful, so perfect. They gave me a bottle and I fed this tiny little fella. He went off to sleep and I sat next to Carol – who was still knocked out at this stage – just praying she was all right and enjoying those first few hours of fatherhood. Finally Carol woke up, but she still wasn't quite with it. She kept saying: "Dan, we made a baby. We made a baby!!" We were so happy. It was so wonderful. We didn't have a clue.

The next day they put us into a private room. It was

fantastic. There were all the phone calls. The flowers were starting to arrive. We were so happy. Then, at about three in the afternoon, a paediatric nurse came into the room and took a little look at Dan, our beautiful boy. As far as we knew up till then, he was perfectly normal, perfectly healthy, a perfect little baby. Our baby.

She looked at him, and then turned around and said quite casually, as if it wasn't in the least bit significant: "Oh, I think this baby has got Down's Syndrome." Just like that. She looked at little Dan, she looked at us and then she went off to get a specialist. She just walked out. Dropped her bombshell, and left.

Carol and I looked at each other, and said: "What?" It was impossible to take in what she'd said. We'd had no warning; nobody had made any mention of Down's at any stage; we couldn't believe our ears. "What does she mean, he's got Down's?"

We looked at our son. He looked absolutely perfect in his hospital cot, oblivious to the chaos of emotions running through us. We thought; "Maybe she's made a mistake." Then in came this other woman, who was a bit more sensitive and sympathetic. She looked at

Dan and said: "I can't confirm it, but looking at your son, he definitely has some of the characteristics of Down's Syndrome."

The signs, she said, were all there. She looked at his hands – children with Down's have lines running straight across their palms. We have breaks in the lines, but with Down's Syndrome the lines go straight across. We looked at Dan's palms, and sure enough the lines ran straight across. His ears too were positioned lower than usual, another classic characteristic. "All the signs are there," she said. "We're going to take some blood tests and we'll be able to confirm the results in three days."

Three days! Can you imagine it? There was no sympathy, no counselling, no tact. It was just: "This is how it is – and you better get on with it." We were completely devastated. All this joy we had had about our beautiful new baby just disappeared; it vanished, went out of the window. In a matter of minutes our world had turned upside down and we had no idea what the future held. I'd always felt so in control of my life; I knew what I wanted and I knew how to get it. Suddenly that sense of control was utterly taken away from me and I didn't know where we were heading. I looked at little Dan. He seemed so perfect to me, so unspoilt, so beautiful. I could scarcely believe what I was being told.

***

It was a terrible, terrifying time. The hospital staff gave us a couple of leaflets about Down's Syndrome, which didn't really offer a great deal of information. We just didn't know what was going on or what we were supposed to think. Then one particularly insensitive nurse came in and said: "It's not so bad. Some of them live till they're eleven or twelve." Just like that. And then she walked out. Not only did we have a child with Down's Syndrome, but from what we were being told, we had a child who could not be expected to live beyond the age of twelve.

While all this was going on, little Danny was in and out of the special baby care unit because he had jaundice. Carol was bed-bound after the Caesarean, barely able to move. She couldn't do anything for Danny, she was in such pain, so it was all up to me.

Poor little Dan. They were sticking needles in him left, right and centre. Every time they put a needle in, I would make sure I was there and I would stroke the back of his neck. Very quickly he grew to expect my fingers, so every time the incubator went up, he would put his hand behind his head, waiting for my finger to stroke him.

We bonded massively in those first seven days. I really looked after that boy. The things they did to him. It was enough to make your heart break. But he just kept looking out for me all the time. That's why he is the way he is with me now. I'm the one he wants; he's always looking out for me. We've got something very special.

It took about three days for the hospital to confirm that Danny had Down's Syndrome. It didn't really sink in. Then they were worried he had a hole in his heart. So Carol, myself and little Dan, still in an incubator, were bundled into an ambulance and taken to Great Ormond Street Children's Hospital in central London to see a heart specialist.

It was such a painful time. Just a few days earlier, we had been like any other young couple. Happy, excited, expecting our baby and looking forward to going home and being a family. Then you find yourself in the middle of a nightmare. Not only has your child got Down's Syndrome, he may have a life-threatening heart condition. You just don't expect all this. It doesn't come into the plan.

**

We saw the specialist. He carried out all his tests and we were told there was nothing wrong with little Dan's heart. Amid all of our problems, suddenly there was a bit of good news. Many children with Down's suffer from problems with their heart, kidneys, eyes and ears. So in many respects we were very lucky. There was light at the end of this very dark tunnel we were travelling through. A feeble shaft of light, but at least it was something.

Before he was born, we had decided our baby was going to be another "Dan Mardell". It would be Danielle if it was a girl, and Dan if it was a boy. There was no argument. That was the way it was going to be. I just wanted another Dan. But when he was born and we found out he had Down's, I'm ashamed to say it now, but I wondered whether I wanted him to be called after me. I remember thinking: "Do we call him Danny, because he's going to have my name for the rest of my life?"

I didn't feel comfortable about it, but Carol insisted she wanted him to be called Dan. She also wanted him to have her father's name, Ivor, as a middle name, but it would have meant that Dan's initials were DIM, which we didn't fancy much given the circumstances. So we settled on Daniel Brandon Mardell.

During that long first week in hospital one of the worst things was having to tell friends and family that our son had Down's Syndrome. We had loads of visitors. All of our friends came, and they walked in with this expectation that we had a healthy, normal child. Then to have to tell them that he had Down's Syndrome and wait for their reaction was very hard.

Astonishingly, the reaction was fantastic from virtually everyone. Perhaps they were very good actors, but they walked in, we told them and they said: "So what?" All of a sudden lots of people started rallying behind us, which was very important.

Apart from that awful first experience with the medical staff, the hospital were very good to us, too. They let me stay there for the week; they put up a bed in Carol's room and I would stay the night, leaving the hospital for about an hour each day to go home, have a shower and a sleep. Then it was back to Whipps Cross, and Carol, and my baby.

They were terrible times. I found it very hard going back to our house. I felt really low. It was then that it really started to hit home – the reality of our situation. While we were in the hospital, we were protected from the outside world. I played the role perfectly of a loving husband and first-time father, but inside it was killing me.

One night the staff asked Carol if she'd like to go out for a couple of hours just to get out of the hospital, and they'd look after Dan. We thought it was a great idea and went out for a curry with Carol's sister and brother-in-law. It should have been a fantastic time, but it wasn't. We were all sad. It was like a kick in the nuts.

We were crying our eyes out every night. I used to lie on my bed, which was lower than Carol's and we would hold each other's hands. The crying got less and less. Carol was fantastic. She adapted very quickly. Like me she was devastated when we were first told, but she wasn't going to have anything said against her child, and after the initial shock it didn't matter to her. During our time at the hospital, I made it look like it didn't matter to me, but I realise now I was grieving terribly.

I remember my dad coming up to the hospital. I told him on the phone and he turned up crying his eyes out, which was the worst thing he could have done. I caught him before he went in the room and I was furious. I told him: "You'd better calm down. You're not going into that room crying. If Carol sees you like that, it's going to be the worst thing you can do."

It was very hard for everyone. My mum came up to the hospital and put on a very brave face, but she admitted to me later that she went home and cried herself to sleep for the next three or four days. I kept going back to see little Dan in the special baby care unit. There were other kids in the unit and I remember looking at my son and feeling ashamed that he wasn't quite right. These other kids only had a bit of jaundice. I kept looking at my boy thinking: "This isn't right. This isn't meant to be happening. It shouldn't be happening to me."

Everything had been going so well for me until then. I'd been having a bit of trouble with the VAT woman – I'd done a few crooked things – but I was on a roll. The business was really taking off and I was making good money. Then along comes Dan. I'd got out of scrapes before, but I couldn't get out of this.

***

Of course I wasn't saying any of this out loud in the hospital. I kept it inside me. I put on a brave face, but deep down I was ashamed of him. I didn't show it to anyone. I wanted to be there for him, and I *was* there for him – at that particular time at least, while I was closeted away in the hospital, cut off from the rest of my world. But it was like I was divorced from reality. Then, when we came out of hospital, things started to go badly wrong.

When we took Dan home, all the nurses turned out

to wish us well and we took all the usual photos that proud new parents take – leaving hospital, getting in the car, Dan in his new car seat. But it was all a show. I went through the motions of being a happy new dad, but really I was totally anti.

After leaving the hospital, we drove straight to my offices in Sugarhouse Lane. We didn't go home, we went straight to where I work. It's strange. I've done it with all three of my children. I suppose I thought, if my son wants to know his dad and find his dad, that was where he would find me, at work. I wouldn't be at home – not for much of the time anyway, I'd be at work. That was my domain. The home was Carol's. So it was really important that I took him to my office first. We took pictures of him sitting on a photocopier. Then I brought him up and showed him off to everyone.

My son. I think everyone was a bit embarrassed for me. They were trying to be natural, but it was all so awkward. Inside I couldn't help thinking that it shouldn't be like this for me. My life isn't like this. It shouldn't be this way.

I kept thinking of how when I was at school I used

to take the piss out of kids with Down's Syndrome and other learning disabilities. How I called them names and made fun of them – like that girl we tried to make drink our urine. I was that kind of boy. And here I was with one of my own. It was like I'd got my just desserts. It was like God had come back to get me. I was deeply, deeply ashamed, of little Danny, and of myself for not being able to love him.

I put on a bloody good show. Nobody would've known. I'm a great bullshitter. I'm a salesman, for heaven's sake. I can make anyone believe anything. But the reality was that I was massively upset. I didn't tell Carol. I just ran away from it; from her, from us, from little Dan. It came out in the months afterwards, but at the time I couldn't tell anyone.

One of the worst moments was going to buy stuff for the baby, from a shop in Leytonstone. It was all meant to be so happy and lovely – buying nappies and sleep suits and bottles and buggies. I went in the shop and they asked me: "Is everything all right with your little boy?"

I just let rip. I couldn't help myself. "No it isn't all right. He's got fucking Down's Syndrome!" That's literally what I said to them and I said it really nastily. It was like an explosion. I remember seeing their faces drop, and thinking: "What are you going to do about that then?"

For a long time we had very little information about Down's Syndrome. We weren't really ready to find out much at that stage. It takes parents quite a long time to come to terms with what's happened and start to contact organisations like the Down's Syndrome Association. They have to get used to the situation first, then they want to know more.

There wasn't much help available at the hospital. There was one midwife there who was particularly helpful. She had a nine-year-old daughter with Down's. She came to see us and the next day she brought in photos of her daughter, which was very thoughtful. She made life a little easier for us. She told us all about her daughter, how she loved fish and chips, and about her friends, and made us realise that she was a real person, not just "someone with Down's". A real child. Just like Dan.

We simply had no idea what life was going to be like with Danny – would he just sit in the corner and do nothing? We didn't have a clue, and that lady helped a lot.

I've since helped raise money to produce a book called *Just Kids*, which is really just a collage of photographs of children with Down's Syndrome, which is available to all new parents of children with Down's. It's a really beautiful little book, showing children at different ages, involved in different activities, to give new parents a better idea of what life is like bringing up a child with Down's and what such children can achieve. It's much more positive than the material we were given and it's now available at most maternity units in the UK. So when a parent finds out they've got a child with Down's, they're given a copy of *Just Kids*.

There was nothing like that for us in those early days after Danny was born, and we weren't ready to find it out for ourselves. The hospital didn't give us much and we didn't seek any more. I found it all too painful to read. We came home and muddled our way through. And that's when things started to go seriously wrong. Within days. I threw myself into my work. I've always worked hard anyway, but it was obvious to everyone that I was trying to avoid facing up to the reality of Dan and my new family. I started working even harder, I wasn't bothered about coming home, not to see Carol, not to see Dan. I used work, and the socialising side of business, as an excuse for not coming home and I started getting drunk in a big way.

I was pissed a lot of the time. I'd start early, at lunch, then I'd drink all the way through, and I just wouldn't go home. At the end of the day I couldn't walk half the time. When I did make it home I had to be dragged into the house. Sometimes I'd forget my keys, so I'd have to bang on the door or ring up to try to get Carol to let me in. Sometimes I'd crash out before I could get through the door. Carol would find me the next morning, slumped in the porch, in the hallway, just inside the door or under the willow tree in our garden. Carol meanwhile was bringing up little Danny single-handedly. They were left on their own much of the time. I was running away. It was a terrible time, but after my experience in the hospital with Dan, it was Carol's time for bonding with him.

Dan needed a lot of help at that time. Every time he cried, I thought it was because he had Down's. I didn't realise he was just a normal baby. The worst thing was putting him in a pram and walking up Wanstead High Road, because we knew a lot of people and they were always looking in the pram. I used to think people were staring at my child. I used to think to myself: "What are you staring at?" They still do it now, but the difference is I don't care. Back then it was more of an embarrassment than a pleasure to be with Dan.

I had to take him to the pub to wet the baby's head. I did all the stuff you're meant to do, but it didn't feel right. We had a christening at the church in Wanstead, and a band in the garden – the full works. It was a great piss-up. But then, when everyone left and the party was over and it was just me and Carol and the baby, I realised it was all false.

Carol was phenomenal. She went out and bought him all these nice clothes. Whatever Dan needed, Dan got. We were beginning to argue about him and I remember one day she shouted at me: "If his own father can't love him, who can? He needs you." I remember her saying that. And I remember thinking, "I may be an ignorant idiot, but I can't love him. I just can't."

I'd bonded with him brilliantly in the hospital; I'd really looked after him, I suppose because Carol couldn't. But outside it was totally different. I even thought about him dying. I thought: "If he died, would it be for the better? What if he had a terminal illness? So, we had a Down's child, but then he was no longer with us? A little bit of heartache, and it's gone." I'm ashamed to admit it, but that's what I thought.

BEHAVING BADLY

I considered leaving Carol and letting her get on with it. I've spoken to other people who've been through what we went through, and now I know lots of people react like I did. I started blaming her. I thought maybe Down's was in her family, maybe it was something in her genes. Then I found out that, somewhere along the line, Ronnie, my older brother, had lost a child. I wondered whether it was my family. It can be hereditary.

Once you have one Down's child there's a very good possibility you are going to have another, the risk is much higher. And when we had our other two children, Frankie and Pia, they tried hard to make us have amniocentesis. We didn't. What would we have done if we'd found another child of ours had got Down's? Would we have got rid of it? We couldn't have. It would have been like rejecting Dan. So there was no point in knowing.

Anyway, as I say, after Danny's birth, I behaved very badly. I wasn't coming home. I didn't want to talk to anyone. All my mates were telling me how brave I was, but I never told them how I really felt. In those early weeks and months, my contact with Danny was very limited. I would feed him now and again, not very often. I didn't want to change him but then again, I've never liked changing any of our three kids. I'm just not good that way.

But with Danny, Carol got no support from me at all. When she'd ask me to come home on time, I'd tell her I was busy and if she'd wanted a bloke like that, she should have married someone who worked at Ford's. I told her I wasn't your average bloke and she'd have to put up with it. Of course, I could have come home if I'd wanted. I just didn't want to face up to

Danny. I didn't want to be there. I hated coming back, to our beautiful house, with that beautiful little nursery we'd made for our baby. We'd had it all done up so it was perfect. And here was my son, who wasn't perfect. It all felt false. All I could think was: "Here's this lovely little nursery, and Danny doesn't even know what's going on around him. We might as well put him in a box in a corner, he wouldn't know." I know it sounds awful, but that's how I felt then.

Carol by this time had started meeting other parents and getting more information about Down's Syndrome. When she brought it home for me to read I'd start the first page and put it down. I couldn't bear it. She was moving on; coming to terms; she was in love with our little boy. I was still at the stage of thinking: "This ain't my son."

When I had Dan in the car with me, I even thought about driving into the river with him. It was like he'd spoilt everything, everything I'd planned for and worked for. It's selfish, I know. I wasn't thinking about anyone else but me. I wasn't thinking of Carol, I wasn't thinking of Dan, I was thinking about me. I do look after myself, that's the way I am. But I was so big-headed I didn't want to admit he was my child. Other parents have told me they've felt the same thing so many times – they just didn't want to admit it because you feel ashamed of those feelings. You grieve for the child you never had, because you end up with something completely different.

One day, when Danny was about seven months old, we did a print show at Wembley. I told Carol I had to stay overnight and that night I got off with some woman. It was just a one-off. I came home in the morning drunk and Carol found out I'd taken this woman to Langan's. She found the receipt in my wallet.

How stupid was that? We had this massive argument and all of a sudden I realised I was going to lose her. It really brought me up sharp. I remember this awful fight I had with her. She was jumping up and down on the bed and she was hitting me with a belt, yelling at me: "He's only seven months old. How can you do this to us?"

She wanted to leave me, and who could blame her, considering my behaviour since Danny's birth? She moved out, took the baby, and went to live with her brother. She was there about two weeks, but I knew I wanted her back. I called every day, apologising to her, promising I would never behave like that again. I convinced her that I was a changed man and – thank God – she came home.

And I did change. True, I was more worried about losing Carol than losing Danny, but it did alter me. I started coming home more; I stopped a lot of the drinking and we started doing things together more as a family.

Little Danny was starting to change, too. In the beginning he was really, really slow to develop. For the first year he didn't do much at all really. And that was the time I wasn't interested in him. He was really floppy because of poor muscle tone. Other kids at the age of one would be up doing things, but Danny couldn't. He fed and slept and that was it. We propped him up with a cushion, and he'd be there with his tongue hanging out.

Then someone told Carol that if she flicked his tongue, he'd put it in. It worked. She didn't like doing it, but she thought she'd be helping him in the long run. Now he never sticks it out, unless he's really concentrating.

All of a sudden, he started doing things. He started sitting up, he started trying to talk. Suddenly he was no longer this floppy kid who couldn't do anything, he was a little boy who was trying to move and talk to me.

At about fourteen months he started sitting up by himself. And when he was two he started trying to talk. His first word was "Dad", or "Dada". Can you believe it? Then he started shuffling round on his bum. He never crawled. That's how I did it as a kid – my mum says I never crawled, I shuffled. It was really good to see him shuffling.

Then, when he was about two and a half, he started walking around, holding on to the furniture. It was amazing. It all suddenly kicked in. It was like, wow. For such a long time he had done nothing, then suddenly everything started to happen at once. He really started developing. And bit by bit, slowly, slowly, I started to fall in love with him.

LEARNING CURVE

It didn't happen overnight, I didn't all of a sudden bond with this boy, but as he struggled, it made me realise he was trying to have a go. He wasn't just sitting in a corner, he was making an effort. And he was recognising me, he was reacting to me. And then gradually I started feeling real love for him. But it was a very gradual process. In hospital I had wanted to protect him and Carol. It was just us against the world. But when I had to face the world with my little boy, it all fell apart. Weird, isn't it? I didn't hate him, I just didn't love him as much as I should have loved him.

It took a long time. Instead of spending my time at work and in the pub, I started wanting to be with Dan. It was Dan himself that changed me. As I got to know him, it was impossible not to love him. He's such a phenomenal kid. I remember him trying to walk. He did three or four steps towards us; he was walking and laughing, and he knew how clever he was being. It was a fantastic moment. Dan was laughing and Carol and I were crying. I'll never forget that.

As I became more interested in Dan, I started wanting to know more about Down's Syndrome and learning disabilities and what lay ahead for my boy. When he was about a year old, Carol contacted the Down's Syndrome Association.

Before that I hadn't really wanted to think about Down's, I don't think. I was still coming to terms with it. I didn't want things about Down's arriving through the letter box. It was a horrible reminder. And, what I read in them, I couldn't fit with Danny. That's not my boy, I used to think. But I think Carol found it really helpful.

Carol was taking him to mother and toddler

groups. Then she found a playgroup we liked – the Buxton Bears playgroup at Chingford – and at the age of two years, ten months we left him for the first time. It was a momentous occasion. They were really, really good with him.

It took a long time to get him out of nappies, which was quite difficult. Danny wasn't really dry until he was five, and then when he was six, he was dry during the night. He's just a bit slower than everyone else to reach these different milestones.

We didn't apply for his disability allowance until he was one and a half. Partly because it's so bloody complicated, partly because I don't think we wanted to face up to it. It wasn't finalised until he was three – it's that difficult. We've just had to do it again, because you have to do it every seven years. It's really hard work. It's question after question after question. How much time do you spend dressing him the morning? How much time do you spend eating? But it's worth it.

Then there's the disabled parking ticket. They ask, "Well, how far can Danny walk?" Which is a tricky one because he can walk, but then he starts complaining about his knees. We've been to doctors and specialists and nobody can see anything wrong. But you have to have a doctor's report to get the ticket. But it's fantastic going into the West End and parking right outside Selfridges – for nothing!

Carol meantime had joined the Redbridge support group of the Down's Syndrome Association. She used to go off to this place called Kenwood Gardens in Ilford which is for all sorts of special needs, and people meet up there. It was fantastic. They were all young girls, like her, and they were all normal people. We had this vision that all these people who had Down's Syndrome kids were all – I don't know – funny people. But then when we started meeting them, they were all nice normal people.

Carol started talking to the other mothers about speech therapy. We contacted the Sarah Duffin Centre at Portsmouth about the possibility of a speech therapist, and Danny started to receive speech therapy once a week when he was about four. It made an enormous difference. I left all that sort of thing to Carol really. She's the real hero of this story. She did all that sort of thing herself. I didn't do any of it. I've just got a few quid together for charity, that's all I've done.

I only became involved with the fund-raising, and the political side of learning disabilities after a chance meeting at a show in Germany. We were doing a deal with Olympus cameras and I was working with someone called Andrew Dyckoff who, I later found out, was voluntary finance director of Mencap. He was interested in what I had told him about Dan, so he arranged for me to have a lunch with some senior people at Mencap.

At the same time, I agreed I would go on this bike ride to India to raise funds for Mencap. Carol was furious – she thought it was awful that I was whizzing off to India and leaving her to cope at home. But it was a great week. One of the best weeks of my life. While we were there, they asked me to make a speech, because I was someone with direct experience of learning difficulties. Most people there were keen to raise money, but they didn't have any personal experience of dealing or living with someone with a learning disability.

I was not a good speaker at that stage – I'd never really done it before. I'm getting better at it now because I'm getting quite a bit of practice. But back then I wrote some notes. I got up to speak and I just threw the notes away. I told people exactly what I had felt. I told them how it was at the beginning – how awful it felt and how badly I behaved. I told them how Dan is now, and what it means to have a child with a learning disability. By the end of it, they were all in tears.

It was amazing. I felt as though I'd released something. I saw the reaction it got from other people and I felt proud – of Danny and of myself. Everyone came up and told me how inspired they were by what I had said. And I started thinking about it and all of a sudden I was feeling good about my son. Talking about Danny in public had made me feel good.

***

At home, Dan continued to make great progress. And, when he was two, Carol became pregnant again. After the initial shock of having Dan and coming to terms with Down's, we had decided that we wanted to have another child. We knew we wanted to give Dan a brother or sister, someone to be brought up with him, so he had someone to play with and learn from. We wanted another child to help teach Dan how to get on in life. Then Frankie came along – and that was the best thing that ever happened to Dan.

Because we had decided we would not have any tests for Down's, we were absolutely terrified when he was born. I just kept checking him over and over; we kept on asking the hospital staff if he was all right. We were desperate to know that he hadn't got Down's. They told us, no, he hadn't got Down's, he was fine. I asked them to check again and again, and they reassured us again and again.

We felt enormous relief. I was delighted it was another boy and much as I loved Danny, I didn't want another child with Down's. I don't know how I would have dealt with it. I suppose I would have accepted it, but I wanted a "normal" child. It was important to me. I don't know why. But I also felt I was helping Danny. The reason Danny has made such brilliant progress is because Frank has shown him so much. As Frank has developed, Dan has developed with him.

After Frankie, we had our daughter Pia and they've both just accepted Danny for what he is. Dan's their brother, he's not the boy with Down's Syndrome, he's just their brother. They don't think of him as any different. He's just always been there. I've never sat down and explained it to them. We decided not to until they were ready. I think Frank is starting to understand, but we'll just have to see how that develops.

Dan has also been fantastic for them. They are both very loving kids, and I think they've learned that from Dan, because children with Down's are often very loving, so Frank and Pia think it's quite normal to be like that, which is lovely. Kids are very loving anyway, but I think ours our extra loving. They're so used to cuddling Danny and being cuddled by him, they're naturally affectionate.

As Dan's grown up, I've grown up, too. I've started to feel real pride in him. He's made fantastic progress. It's been steady and gradual, but he's done brilliantly.

When he was five, there was a real breakthrough. It was at school sports day and I was so proud of him. We'd been to previous sports days and he'd been included in everything, which was fantastic but he didn't have a clue about what he was supposed to be doing so I'd always helped him through the whole thing.

But that year when he was five, he was in the yellow team and something amazing happened. He did everything on his own. I didn't have to help him at all. It was an amazing feeling, seeing him fitting in with all the other children, doing exactly what he was meant to be doing, without any extra helpers running around organising him. I stood there crying my eyes out, it was so moving, and lots of the other parents were crying as well. They've witnessed our journey and what I felt that day was immense pride for Danny. It was a real milestone.

I love him to bits, but I can still be quite negative about Dan, even now. Like when he decides to take all his clothes off and go for a run. I tell him: "Put your bloody clothes on," but he just laughs at me. We were at a meeting of parents of children with Down's Syndrome the other day, and they told me their kids do exactly the same. They all take their clothes off. Perhaps they don't like wearing clothes, but I get annoyed about it.

And I get annoyed when he does a bunk. He runs

off a lot. It's like he doesn't realise the dangers. We've lost him at Walthamstow dogs before – imagine trying to find your son at Walthamstow dog track on a Saturday night because he's run off. I get very annoyed inside myself, thinking: "Why am I walking around trying to find my son? He should be here. Why doesn't he just stay with me like other kids?"

Some people say Down's kids are stubborn, but they're not. It's just that they like routine, they don't like change. And if you suddenly change their routine, they don't like it. They don't see why they should. You have to sit down and talk and try to explain so they know what to expect. It's like at Centreparks with all the rapids. He really won't want to have a go, but I'll grab him kicking and screaming, and we'll do it, and then he absolutely loves it. But in the beginning he finds new things very difficult to deal with.

Like when I took him to a Formula 1 race – he's one lucky kid, isn't he? First of all he was terrified of the noise and I couldn't get him to move. The next thing you know he's in the car; he's got his earplugs on and he's away. You have to be very careful, to prepare him for any change. And he doesn't sleep very well. It was always like musical beds in our house.

So it's not all plain sailing but we've gained an awful lot from having Dan. Apart from all the love and the fun and the huge learning curve along which we're still travelling, we've gained a whole new world too. I've been to places and met people I never would have met without Danny.

LAUNCHING DANNY'S CHALLENGE

It was after the bike ride with Mencap that I started to become seriously involved in charity work, raising money and increasing awareness about learning disabilities. It wasn't something I sought out for myself. It found me. When the Mencap people returned from India they reported back to the directors about my speech and my personal experience with Danny, and the guy who was head of funding at Mencap at the time invited me to lunch.

I told him I'd be more than happy to get involved with Mencap and he asked me if I would be interested in becoming an ambassador for the charity. An ambassador is someone who goes out, talks about Mencap, shares experiences and helps fund raising. They were trying to appoint ten ambassadors at that time and I was chuffed to be asked. They were asking some quite important people, among them the Tory MP, Archie Norman, who has a brother with Down's Syndrome.

I've known Archie a long time, and I was quite honoured to be asked alongside him to work for Mencap. I was in good company. I felt quite good about it. Unfortunately Archie wasn't able to take up the offer because he had just been made chairman of the Conservative Party and had a lot on his plate, which was a pity. The whole thing went a bit quiet for a while. I had a lot on; my business was doing very well, and I was extremely busy. But in the spring of 2001 I contacted Mencap again and suggested having another chat to see what we could sort out. So I went to see them and we banged around some ideas.

We went back to this idea of me being an ambassador. I was told it would involve going to functions, making speeches and raising money. I asked how much

I would be expected to raise and they said they'd never had an individual raise £100,000 in twelve months. Did I think I could do it? "Yeah," I said casually. "I'll do that," as if it was no big deal. "I'll raise you a hundred grand. That would be a bit of a challenge wouldn't it?" And that's where the name Danny's Challenge came from.

I said yes to it, just like that. It was only when I got in my car that I thought: "Shit! How on earth am I going to raise £100,000 in twelve months?" It suddenly hit me that it was a hell of a lot of money and I began to think I'd bitten off more than I could chew.

So that was the beginning of the whole thing. Mencap appointed a little committee to work with me, including someone from fund-raising and someone from marketing, and we sat down to work out how to get this fund-raising off the ground. We thought up all the usual things – a Danny's Challenge ball; a Danny's Challenge golf day; Carol and I decided to do Mencap's China bike ride.

We worked on it for a bit, but I began to feel uncomfortable with the set-up. It became obvious fairly early on that we were not going to gel very easily, me and Mencap. They like doing things their way, I like doing them my way, and we were very, very different.

For example, I decided I was going to have a launch party for Danny's Challenge at the Atlantic Bar in central London in October 2001. It's not the sort of thing Mencap would have done, but it was absolutely fantastic. I paid for it myself; it got loads of publicity and plenty of press and celebrities came along. I'm good friends with a guy called Keith Bishop who's an agent so he got lots of celebs to come along to raise the profile of the event. There were actors from *Coronation Street* and *Hollyoaks*; Archie Norman was there, so was Michael Cole, the old BBC royal correspondent who went to work for Mohammed Al Fayed.

It was a brilliant night. I'll never forget it. Little Dan was there. I gave a speech, talking a bit about Danny and about our attitudes to people with Down's Syndrome and other learning difficulties. I normally speak off the cuff, but on this occasion I'd written down what I wanted to say and it completely shocked everyone in the room. It had an extraordinary impact. I don't think they'd ever heard anything like it before. I confronted them with their own prejudices. I reminded them of all the awful names we used to call people with learning difficulties when we were children. We've all done it – "mong", "div", "village idiot", "silly kid"… I told them I'd done the same myself, but now I had a child of my own with Down's Syndrome. It had been a long journey for me, I told them, but I'd now realised that people with learning disablities had just the same rights as anyone else and they deserved exactly the same respect. Everyone just stood there. I could see people thinking: "Oh my God, this is how I used to talk."

Mencap were there that night, but the relationship between us was fast deteriorating. We worked in entirely different ways. So I just got on with it on my own. I started setting up my own committees, a Danny's Challenge ball committee and a Danny's Challenge golf day committee. We held a meeting at the Marriott Hotel in Grosvenor Square to discuss the ball and we had a serious falling out with

Mencap about how it should be organised. It all started to go downhill very quickly from there.

***

I don't think Mencap liked the way we worked. My dad, who was on one of the committees, had a bit of a go at the two Mencap women who came along to one of our meetings. He doesn't pull any punches, my dad, and they went back to their office and reported that they'd had a very hostile reception. I think I spoke the wrong language for Mencap. Mencap is a huge organisation; it's like a plc charity. We're not plc; we're a limited company from East London. I think they started to wonder whether we were projecting the right image for them.

Then, in October 2001, a friend of mine approached me and asked whether I would like to turn over one of our warehouses at Sugarhouse Lane for a "gentlemen's evening" one night to raise money for charity. The deal was we would split the money between three charities, one of which would be Danny's Challenge.

I thought this sounded like a great idea, so I agreed and we transformed one of the buildings into a beautiful nightclub for the night. We had 38 strippers from all over Europe taking part and 400 blokes paid to come and see. The deal was that my name would not be associated with it, just in case it went wrong, but we'd have a third of the profits for Danny's Challenge.

Well, we made a bundle of money that night. I wasn't sure Carol was going to approve, but she came in for a look and enjoyed it so much we didn't leave until three in the morning. We did an auction and we raised about £27,000 in total, of which a third went to Danny's Challenge. Not bad for an evening's work, but I don't think it was Mencap's cup of tea.

It was then I came up with the idea of boxing to raise money for charity. I'd been to an International White Collar Boxing Association event. A friend called Alex Leitch was fighting for the world title, and that's when it came to me. I watched this fight sat round the table and then turned round to everybody and said: "Right, I'm going to get back in the ring and I'm going to win the British title, and I'm going to raise money for charity!" Everyone just looked at me in disbelief.

There I was – this fat, middle-aged businessman. I weighed nineteen and a half stone, I was totally unfit and I hadn't boxed for years. The last time I had been really fit was when I was twenty-two years old, just back from Saudi Arabia. And I thought I could just jump back in the ring and do the business. You can see why my mates laughed at me. I had a couple more pints and I told them I could do it and I would do it. That's the problem with me. That's how I go through life. I tell everyone, then I have to go through with it. After I'd said it, there was no going back.

I told Mencap about my boxing idea. They didn't like it. They said they weren't sure they wanted to be involved. When I asked why, they said boxing caused brain damage and they didn't think a charity like Mencap should be associated with that. I can see their point, but at the time it really put my back up. I told them more people got hurt in motor racing and rugby than in the boxing ring. It really gave me the hump. I said I was going to go ahead and do the fight, but all the proceeds would go to the Down's Syndrome

Association, who were happy to take the money, rather than Mencap.

Things went from bad to worse. I asked where the £100,000 I was raising was going to be spent, they told me it wasn't my concern. I told them that the sort of people I was working with wanted to know where the money would end up. It all came to a head and I called a meeting and told them we were finished. Danny's Challenge was, from that moment, independent. It was no longer anything to do with Mencap. And that's how Danny's Challenge properly started out.

***

I opened a Danny's Challenge bank account and started up a foundation. I kept the £100,000 target, but we exceeded it within weeks. And I went to see Carole Boyes of the Down's Syndrome Association. They had a completely different approach and it was an inspirational meeting. Their attitude was great and I knew I was finally working with the right people. We were going to get on. I didn't care whether it was Mencap, the Down's Syndrome Association or

Danny's Challenge; I just wanted to inform people about learning disabilities and raise money for charity.

So Mencap and I went our separate ways. We were just different. We are very small and our agenda's completely different. I want as much money as possible from Danny's Challenge to go to the end user, not to go to pay for a vast organisation like Mencap. I don't work like that. I'm doing it in a different way.

The Down's Syndrome Association was completely happy with the boxing idea. All they were concerned about was whether we were going to raise the profile of the association and talk about people with learning disabilities, and they wanted to be sure the money was going to be spent in the right places.

So I began thinking about the boxing idea. How was I going to get this fight publicised? How was I going to let people know that there was this fat businessman who was going to go back in the ring and raise money for charity? And suddenly this brilliant idea came to me. Wouldn't it be great if I got Nigel Benn to corner for me? Nigel and I went to school together. We were enemies at school and used to fight each other all the time. I'm the only man

Nigel Benn has ever been scared of.

We must have had a dozen fights over the years. We were always having a ruck. I remember one in particular. I was sitting down with a couple of mates and Nigel came up – I still don't know why – and he did this karate chop on the back of my neck. He said: "I'm having you at break." I looked at him, and I said: "All right then, I'll have you."

I didn't really want to fight him because he was one hard bastard. You didn't want to fight Nigel Benn. He had a reputation for being really hard, and he just didn't give up. He could really have a ruck. Although we had a few over the years, I never ever enjoyed fighting him. I'd started boxing then, and I was always working in the greengrocers throwing around bags of spuds, so I was quite a strong fella. Nigel's brother, Mark, was in my class. On this particular occasion he came up and said: "I hear you're having Nigel at break?"

I said: "Yeah." He said: "I don't want anything to do with it, it's between you and him." I said: "Fine, stay away."

I'd asked my mate to warn me when Nigel came

down the corridor so I could jump him, but he told me he didn't want anything to do with it. Nobody wanted to be involved because it was Nigel. But I forced my mate do it and told him he could piss off once he'd warned me.

So Nigel's walked down this corridor and, as luck would have it, his parker coat was over his head and his satchel over his shoulder. I jumped out, pulled the coat over his head and yanked the satchel down so his arms were trapped. He couldn't move, and I beat him up. He went down and I remember kicking him in the face and thinking: "Wow, Nigel's on the deck." I walked off and left him there. It was over in seconds.

I went in to the science lab. The doors swung open and Nigel came running in. He's got the scariest eyes, Nigel, especially when he's lost his temper. He came running at me and I picked up one of these heavy lab stools and I smacked him across the head with it. He went down again and I kicked him and that was the end of him. My reputation went up ten-fold. He was off school for a week. He came back and he stayed out of my way until we were in the break area.

I was a flash git at school. Because I was working at

this greengrocers, I had a nice few quid in my pocket. I was earning about £18 a week, which was quite a lot of money then, especially for a schoolkid, and I was spending all my money on my clothes. And there I was at school wearing an antelope skin jacket.

At break Nigel got me in an area where there was nothing to pick up to defend myself. I was looking at him. I wasn't scared. I jumped straight into him and we were like two cats spinning around. It really went off. My jacket ended up torn to shreds. He ended up with no shirt on his back. We probably fought for three or four minutes which is a long time to fight, and the teachers wouldn't try to break it up because we were a couple of tough kids. They were too scared to get involved. Two sixth formers, both tough kids who were boxers too, finally jumped in and tried to break it up.

They pulled me off him. I was just completely going mad. They calmed us down and we were put outside the headmaster's office. Nigel was looking at me and I was looking at him, and he said: "Have you had enough?" I said: "Have you had enough?" He said: "I've had enough. Shall we call it a day?" I said,

"I'd love to." And we shook hands and we just laughed at each other. I didn't realise how much respect he had for me.

That's the one great memory I have of Nigel, and he tells people: "This is Danny. He's the guy who bashed me over the head with a chair at school."

I wasn't at school much after that. I was about to leave school to join the forces, so I didn't see Nigel for many, many years, but I followed his progress in the boxing ring. He joined the army and began boxing for them but I didn't see him again until he started boxing professionally. I went to watch him down York Hall in Bethnal Green.

Someone told Nigel I was there, and he asked me to join him in the changing room. This was before he was Nigel Benn the famous boxer. He was so pleased to see me, it was like seeing an old friend. We'd never really been friendly. But he did have a bit of respect for me as a fighter.

So it seemed a brilliant idea all those years later to get Nigel involved with Danny's Challenge. By this time he had already retired from the ring, so I went round to his dad's house in Ilford and asked him to get

Nigel to call me. A few days later I had this phone call. It was Nigel. I told him I needed to come and see him, so one Saturday afternoon in January 2002 we had a meeting at his house in Beckenham in Kent.

It was like talking to an old buddy. We spent two hours in the kitchen having cups of tea and packets of crisps, talking about the old days. He was absolutely flabbergasted to see how fat I was. There I was, 19 and a half stone. He looked at me and said: "What have you done with your bloody life?"

So I told him about Dan, and what Danny's Challenge was all about. He was really interested. Nigel's very religious. He found God and he's got a very caring attitude. He tries to be a good human being. It happens to a lot of boxers. They find religion. I think they're trying to redeem themselves after all they've done.

Anyway, we're having a good old chat and I said to Nigel: "The reason I wanted to talk to you is because I want you to corner me. It would make a great story if I came out and you were in my corner." Nigel sat there. He said: "I ain't cornering you, you fat bastard. I'll train you."

I said: "What?" He said: "I'll train you. I'll get you ready for this fight."

I'm sat there and I didn't know what to think. I couldn't believe what I was hearing. Two times world champion Nigel Benn, all of a sudden, he's not just going to corner me, he's offering to train me. I couldn't believe my luck. I said: "Why? Why are you offering to train me?"

"Because look at the state of you Dan," he said. "If you get in that ring, it's not just you you're representing, it's me. If you get in there, you're going to win and you're going to look good because I'm going to make sure you do."

I just sat there. I couldn't believe how lucky I was, but I was also quite scared. All of a sudden it began to dawn on me what I was doing. Not only was I getting back into the ring, but I'd got one of the best fighters that Britain's ever produced backing me. It was daunting.

Nigel took me to the bottom of his garden where he had this gym. He showed me where we were going to do the training. He said: "Right, I want you to come over on Monday. I'm going to buy you a plastic suit."

I'd never heard anything like it. He said we were going to do an hour and a half every day in the gym, and he was going to put the heating up to ninety degrees to help me lose some of the weight.

He asked to see me on the bags. I showed him what I could do, and it was like: "Oh My god, what the hell have I done?" Then he showed me what he could do on the bags, and I was in awe. There I was in Nigel Benn's gym and he's hitting the bags in front of me. People would pay money for this! And he was going to train me to fight! I left Nigel's house walking on air. I could hardly believe my luck. It was a godsend – the biggest PR story I could have hoped for. I went straight round my dad's to tell him. He couldn't believe it.

***

Nigel's wife was a bit wary of me at first. I think you do become wary when you are that successful. Normally people are trying to get something out of you. But I was different. I turned up at Nigel's house in my Bentley. I was already very successful myself as a businessman.

"I took one look at you and realised that you don't need anything from me," Nigel said. "You've got as much money as me and you've got more going on in your life than I have. I knew I wouldn't have a problem working with you."

The other thing he said was that he knew that I would do it. He said: "I remember your attitude at school and you're a winner, you don't give up and you're ex-forces. That's how I knew you'd do it." He's ex-forces too, so he knows how we think and we think the same. If we say we're going to do something, we'll get it done.

Nigel was a bit reluctant to get involved in the PR side of things at first – he's a very private man – but I knew how important it was. I contacted a PR company and they got into it straight away. They contacted all the sports journalists from the nationals. It all took off in a big, big way. That bit was easy – getting people interested in our story. The hard bit was getting me ready for the fight. Never mind Danny's Challenge, what about Nigel Benn's challenge? How on earth was he going to transform this fat old businessman into a fighting machine?

I was badly overweight. I'd spent years drinking too much and eating too much. To tell you the truth I was a real pisshead before Danny's Challenge took over my life. It was my lifestyle. I would do two or three big lunches a week. I'd go to Langan's and before the meal I'd have five or six gin and tonics. At the table I'd always drink the best wines. As soon as we sat down, I'd order a premier cru and I'd order a bottle of the best red. The bottle would be empty before the starter had even arrived. As soon as we'd finished lunch, if the customer had to go, I'd go back to the bar and find someone else to have a drink with.

I'd have twenty to twenty-five drinks in a day maybe. I made everyone else keep up with me. I used to get the hump if people couldn't keep up. But before we'd even sat down for dinner they'd be smashed.

My boozing was particularly bad in those first months after Danny was born. I think I was on the verge of alcoholism. But even after I came to terms with what had happened, I was still a heavy drinker. I still like the best restaurants, the best hotels, the best food, the finest wines. But back then I thought the only way to do business was to go out and get drunk.

I enjoyed it for about ten years, so by the time I embarked on Danny's Challenge I was very over-weight and very unfit.

Then in November 2001 I had a serious wake-up call. I was buying some more property and as part of the deal I had to have a medical through the insurers. I thought it would be absolutely routine, but after they checked me out I was refused insurance. The insur-ance company wrote and told me to go and see a doc-tor. I was terrified. I thought I had cancer or some-thing.

It was about six weeks before Christmas when I went to see the doctor. He said: "Do you drink a lot?" I said: "Yeah, I drink for England." He said: "Do you eat a lot?" I said: "Yeah, and I eat all the wrong foods." He said: "You're seriously overweight, your liver's knackered, you've got high blood pressure and you drink too much. At this stage everything's reversible. Your liver, if you give it six months, will rebuild. But if you carry on the way you have been, you are not going to make old bones. You are leading the wrong kind of life."

It was devastating. And the timing was amazing.

Just as I'm thinking of getting back into the ring, the doctor tells me I'm heading for the grave. That was it. I told the doctor there and then that I was going to get utterly pissed for the next six weeks, up to Christmas. Then I would get myself fit. And that's what I did. In the run-up to Christmas I drank non-stop. It was probably the heaviest drinking I've ever done. I just binged. I think I wanted to get it out of my system. Then in January 2002 everything changed. I stopped.

I hadn't had a drink for four or five days and I went to the gym for the first time. I thought it would be easy. I thought: "I'm Danny Mardell, I can do whatever I like." Carol tried to warn me I needed to be fitter to get in the ring, but as usual, I thought I knew best. I started going to the Kronk gym in Camden Town where Lennox Lewis used to train. After about 20 minutes working on the bags, I started to feel sick. I was just drained of energy. It was awful. I started thinking: "Shit, what on earth have I got myself into. I'm in the ring and I'm just a fat old bloke." I was starting to realise just how much of a mountain I had to climb. I think I was kidding myself, that I would be able to get fit and fight, while still drinking and living the life I had been leading. No way. It quickly became clear to me there was absolutely no chance of that.

I felt really awful that first time in they gym. But it didn't make me feel like giving up. If anything it made me feel even more determined. I drove home and told Carol: "That's it. I'm not drinking any more." I set myself a goal to lose one and a half stone. I was nineteen and a half stone at that time. Five months later I was fighting at 15st 1lb.

***

Little Danny – the whole reason for all this – was meanwhile making fantastic progress. He stayed at playgroup until he was five, then we had to find him a school, which was terrifying. Not a lot of schools at that time already had Down's Syndrome children. It's a bit different now. There are more children in the mainstream system. When we were looking for Danny it was still pretty rare to find Down's children in mainstream classes, but we were determined that's what we wanted for him.

So we went to look at our local school. It looked

perfect. It was really small, a beautiful little place in the woods – it was like a dream school, just the sort of place you'd want your kids to go to. It was near where we lived, we were in the catchment area. But as soon as we walked in we knew instantly that it wasn't right. We took Danny to visit with us and the head teacher didn't even look at him. She was very off-hand. She said she had no facilities for him.

We asked her what she meant, what special facilities he needed, and she said the school had no shower facilities. We asked why he needed shower facilities, and she said if he had an accident. Carol told her he was dry and out of nappies. But she insisted that the school down the road had a shower and he might be better off there. We asked her what she did if any of the other children had an accident and she said she called the parents. We said: "Well, why can't you call us if Danny has an accident?"

In the end we just walked out. I told her: "We're not wasting our time here. You obviously don't want our son in your school. We're leaving." And we marched off. Straight out. I was absolutely furious. It was awful. She utterly ignored him. It was obvious she didn't want him in her school, and we certainly didn't want him there. It was the first time we had encountered any real prejudice against him, and the last. We've experienced nothing like it since. It was terrible. We felt quite hurt.

We went to see other schools which weren't quite right for him. There was one where the head teacher was really scary – *I* was terrifed of her! We couldn't send him there. We finally found the right place for him at a lovely school called Buckhurst Hill County Primary near Loughton in Essex. Carol rang the head teacher, Mrs Lesley Howes, and we knew straight away – even before going to see the school – that it was the place for him. Just the tone of her voice and what she said. We told her Danny was Down's Syndrome and she said: "Oh yes, absolutely no problem at all. Come along and see us." You could just hear it in her voice. She was so welcoming.

So we went along and it was fantastic. Everything we had hoped for him. Mrs Howes was fantastic with him. She spent a lot of her time talking to him, not talking to us. She gave all her attention to him; it was wonderful. She showed him around and introduced him to everyone. We said there and then: "Yes, we want him to come here." There was no going away and making minds up. This was it.

And Danny has never looked back. When he first started, Mrs Howes introduced him during assembly. She invited him up onto the stage and told the children: "This is a very special boy called Danny. Everybody in this school is going to look after him." And they do. The whole school love him. We've had no problems at all, either with children or parents. One of our friends who's got a child with Down's put her kid in another mainstream school, and she's had awful problems with parents coming up to her and saying "Your kid shouldn't be in this school."

But we've never had that with Dan. When he first started all the kids were fighting with each other over him. They all wanted to play with him. Now he's got a lovely group of friends he plays with at school and out of school at each other's houses. He plays a lot with the big boys and they all come up to him and say: "All right Danny, respect!" Everyone says hello to him when they see him. They don't say hello to me. He's very happy and doing very well. He actually runs into school, he's so happy to be there. He was in a little play they put on at the school the other week, where he welcomed everyone and thanked everyone for coming. He did brilliantly.

He has a full time worker with him in class, which has been great. And he's really concentrating. He still runs off a lot. But to see him do things like any other kid – this year especially – has been fantastic. There's alot of things he can't do – he wants to go to tennis, because Frankie goes to tennis, but he can't. He wants to go to football, but we tried that and he runs off. Carol's got him into gymnastics now. Videos and TV he'll watch forever if you let him. Though that's probably true of all children. And he really loves history, like Henry VIII, and knights and castles. The Tower of London is his favourite place to go. My mum takes him a lot to those kind of places. They get on brilliantly. And he loves all the Danny's Challenge stuff. When he meets someone he says: "Hello, I'm Danny's Challenge". He's one very, very clever kid. He isn't what you expect at all. I think he's fantastic, but then I would, wouldn't I?

TRAINING, AND THE FIGHT

After my first meeting with Nigel, training began in earnest. It was crazy. I was training three times a day. Before work I'd meet up with Jerry Jackson, a fitness trainer for twenty years, who started to get me into shape. I'd arrive in the office, have a shower, check what needed doing, then jump in the car and dash down to Beckenham to train with Nigel. Then in the evening I'd be at a gym in Dagenham sparring.

Nigel was tough. Very tough. But he had to be. The first day of training I arrived. He told me he hadn't managed to get me the plastic suit, but he'd cut out a bin liner for me to wear. He told me to take off all my clothes and put it next to my skin, then put my training kit on top. I looked at him and said: "Are you sure?" Then he got me on the scales. I'm standing there starkers and he weighs me. I'm nineteen and a half stone. He said: "This is the deal Dan. Two strikes and you're out. I'm going to weigh you on a Monday and weigh you on a Friday. If you go up in weight twice, I'm walking away from the training. You've got to start losing weight. We've got to get that weight off you and we've got to do it quickly."

What an incentive it was. He changed my diet, he bought me a lorry load of vitamins. I still take them – twenty-four tablets a day. Echinacea, glucosamine, calcium magnesium, amino acids, vitamin C, EPA fish oil (three twice a day), pharmaton. He put me on fat metabolisers to break down the fat in my body.

"This is science," he said. "You want to train like a world champion, this is what you've got to do."

Carol couldn't believe it when she saw all the bottles. "What are you, a drug addict?" she said.

That first day, dressed in my bin liner, we went into Nigel's gym. It was ninety degrees, the music was cranked right up and it was fantastic. Nigel got hold of me, laid me down on the floor and began climbing all over me – stretching me like I've never been stretched, pulling me from pillar to post and putting me into positions I didn't even know I could get into. All the time, he was talking to me, explaining to me what he was doing and why he was doing it. I came out of there completely and utterly knackered.

Some days I went round there and he'd take me for a run round the golf course. Then we'd go back in the gym and do an hour in there. It was amazing. It was a privilege. I used to get almost embarrassed going down there, thinking: "Am I messing this guy's life up? Am I taking liberties with this man's life?"

We bonded very well; we became very friendly, but it took a little time for it to happen. He didn't want money. People would pay thousands for that experience, but he wasn't in it for the money. He's not that sort of character. All he wanted was that once I said I'd do it, I had to do it well and on his terms. In the end, Carol and I became good friends with Nigel and his family. He knew I didn't want anything off him, and that's why we got on so well. Within a couple of weeks he invited me to join him at the Pride of Britain awards. Then he started taking me to film premières.

I took the training really seriously. I called in all my staff and told them they wouldn't be seeing much of me for the next four months. I told them they'd have to run the company themselves and do a good job, because the most important thing to me at that moment was winning the fight. I told them I didn't give a shit about the company at that moment. The fight was everything.

I became very, very focused. I must have become unbearable to live with. As soon as I ate something, before the plates were even cleared away, I'd put on my shoes to go for a walk, because Nigel told me, as soon as you've eaten don't sit down, walk it off. I became this consummate professional fighter. That's how I lived for five months.

The weight started falling off. Every day I was four or five pounds lighter. I started thinking "I can do this." I was changing beyond recognition. It took over my life. But who was I going to fight?

The guy that runs the International White Collar Workers Boxing Association (ICWBA) – it trades in the UK as the Real Fight Club – is a promoter called Alan Lacey. I went to see him and told him what I wanted to do. We agreed the deal. He would put on six fights. He'd find the other fighters and he would organise the boxing side of it, the ring and medical requirements. He gave me some tapes of other heavy weights – a couple of guys called Alex Leitch and Lee Short – to help me find an opponent.

I thought at that stage I would get down to seventeen stone, so Leitch and Short looked like fair opponents. Never in my wildest dreams did I think I would get to fifteen stone. I watched the tapes and I decided I wanted to fight Leitch. I was thinking about the PR spin. He's a city lawyer. I put the whole thing together in my mind – a fat millionaire businessman, a smart city lawyer and boxing legend Nigel Benn What a fantastic story.

A week later I bumped into Leitch at a boxing do and asked him if he was up for it. He looked me up and down and I had my opponent. He was fantastic. He got involved in all the PR; he did interviews with papers. We started being filmed for a Yorkshire Television documentary about Danny's Challenge and Alex couldn't have been more helpful. He was brilliant. And he trained really hard. He sussed out that it was a good opportunity for him, too. Without being big-headed, these are glorious nights for my opponents too. They get such exposure out of it. People want to fight me, because they get that publicity.

These days I'm quite a tactician in the ring. I used to be a bit of a brawler but I'm getting quite good now. I've fought quite a few times since that first Danny's Challenge fight, and my skills have improved no end. But that first fight, I was a real scrapper. It was terrible. A real ruck.

***

Nigel trained me for five months solid. It was an amazing time. All of a sudden, once the story was out, it became very busy. Not only was there all the training, we ended up with two documentaries running simultaneously. I had two different film companies working with me. In addition to the Yorkshire TV documentary, a programme called *Fitness Files* was filming me. They were interested in the training, so they were following me around, coming to the house, coming running with me. Not only did we have all the pressure of the training and the fight, now we had two film crews on tow. Our lives were turned upside down. Carol and I would get up in the morning and we'd have TV crews all over the house. Then I'd get *Talk Sport* ringing me up, asking me to go down to do radio interviews for BBC Radio 5. It was mad. But I loved it. I've got to be honest, I LOVED it.

Work suffered quite badly. Turnover went down a lot. It came back afterwards, but it did suffer. It took a lot out of us all – Carol and I were arguing – it was all very pressurised, but little Dan loved it. He's a superstar, Dan. It didn't phase him one bit.

You wouldn't think it, but I really did get quite nervous. I'm not normally the nervous type but I was very worried about getting in the ring. I was worried about my stamina, whether I was fit enough for it. I was worried I wouldn't win. I was worried whether I would make a fool of myself.

The ticket sales had gone fantastically well. I'd put myself up for it, now I had to walk the walk.

The date for the fight was 16 May 2002. It loomed very quickly. Before I knew it, it was the night before. I decided that I didn't want to stay at home so I went to stay at my dad's in Wapping. It was a bad idea. The bedroom he gave me was on the roadside, not the riverside. There were no curtains and I spent the whole night worrying about the fight. I got absolutely no sleep at all. So the next morning I was knackered, and very, very nervous.

Then something funny happened. When I got to the venue that evening, it all went. My nerves completely disappeared. I made a decision that I would give a speech before my fight, to explain Danny's Challenge to everyone. Nigel went absolutely mad. He told me he didn't want me doing that at all. He said I was there to have a fight – not to give speeches. That's the professional in him. But I was determined. I wanted to meet everyone, say hello and explain what was going on. All the family was in the audience, including little Dan, of course. And he loved every bit of it.

It was a proper dinner do with five hundred guests. So about half way through people's meals, I came out and went round saying hello to them. Then I went in the ring and did the speech.

It was the speech I'd given all those months earlier, at the start of this whole journey – cycling in India for Mencap. I told them how I used to feel about people with learning disabilities. About the prejudices I had when I was younger. About how I used to treat people. All those horrid words. I used those words, and I told them a lot of people there that night would have done so as well.

You could have heard a pin drop. You could see it in their faces, they were really thinking about it. They'd recognised themselves in what I was telling them. "And don't think that it can't happen to you, because it can," I told them: "It happened to me, and it could happen to you and we've got to treat people in a different way."

And it worked. It worked brilliantly. It was a great speech. It really got to them. People were in tears. It obviously worked because of the amount of money people spent afterwards. It was an amazing occasion. It was the best thing I had ever done.

Then I went back to the changing room and that's when it started to get really surreal. I've got Nigel

Benn there. I've got Kevin Leushing, another famous boxer. People that I admire in the world of boxing are sitting in my corner. Out among the crowd there's John Conteh, there's John H Tracey, there's Charlie Magri. All world champions who've come out to see me fight. We had Steve Collins reffing (WBO Super Middle Weight Champion). It had become very, very big.

I'm sitting in the changing room thinking, "Bloody hell fire. What have I gone and let myself in for? How have we got ourselves here in five months?" I'm four and a half stone lighter, I've got five hundred people out there waiting to see me fight and I've got two TV teams out there. I couldn't believe what we had pulled off in such a short space of time. And I was the star of the night, it was just fantastic, but very nerve racking.

We'd planned this great entrance. We could hear the crowd outside, and Nigel was getting excited. I'd got all these big blokes on walkie talkies. We had the hype, the hysteria, it was really happening. Everybody's pulses were racing. I'd got a six-foot-eight-inch bouncer dressed up as a biker as part of my entourage. Then they switched every light off in the arena. It's pitch black apart from one spotlight. The music was pounding – "Can You Feel the Force?" And it was electric.

Everybody went mad – they leapt on their chairs, clapping their hands. Then I came out and I was dancing. It was like, "Wow!" It was fantastic. The nerves weren't there any more. I was kissing people, shaking people's hands. And Nigel came out as cool as custard and said: "Dan, don't talk to people, we're having a fight." Typical Nigel. Everybody's clapping and patting me on the back, and I get in the ring and the poor sod I'm fighting must have looked at all this and thought: "Oh my god!"

First round, I came out and just walked through him. It was a nice scrap, and I was just too strong for him. The training Nigel had given me really showed that night. I was fit and I just beat the guy up. After the first round, he just hung onto me. He was clinging on for dear life. I just walked through his punches and I had a real go at him. He wasn't strong enough for me. I was hitting him. I was banging and banging and banging. I wouldn't let him rest. I won the bloody fight and I won very convincingly. It was a great feeling and I didn't feel sorry for him one bit. I'd earned it.

I was standing there in the ring and everybody was saying: "Dan it's your fight!" I started to get all emotional. It was the culmination of everything, it all started to get on top of me. They went to the judge's scores, and suddenly they said: "The new champion is Danny Mardell. My hand went up and I thought: "I've done it, I've done it."

I get all emotional just thinking about it, even now. After the announcement, little Danny was straight in the ring with me. He was the first person I looked at. I was so proud of him. He was walking around the ring with his hands up and he kept on cuddling me. It was just fantastic. "My dad's the champion," he kept saying. "My dad's the champion."

Frankie came in the ring, Dad came in the ring, Carol was in the ring, and Pia. It was like a world championship fight. There were TV cameras, people clapping and cheering. The atmosphere was electric.

And it's funny, that night it all came back to me why we were doing it, and what people were doing there. As I came out I found out we'd made £60,000. And I realised these people were there because of Danny's Challenge – because of what we were saying about learning disabilities. The fight was important, but so was the occasion, and the reason for the occasion. I felt such a sense of achievement. I was really proud of what we'd done. We'd done something quite special. I came away that night feeling really quite proud of myself, and of little Dan.

In the real world, my feelings for Danny were getting stronger and stronger. Throughout the whole thing – the fight, the PR and the TV documentaries – he conducted himself brilliantly. He just captured people's hearts. Even now I look at Danny a bit differently every day – there's always some new achievement. The way he handles life. Every day you love him more.

***

After the fight it was a massive anti-climax. I went on the piss for a few days as per usual. We all went away on holiday to Portugal. I thought: "Right I've done it." I'd done what I set out to do. Of course, Danny's Challenge went on. We had a golf day to organise, but then I wasn't that interested. That personal challenge I'd set myself, to get fit, to get back in the ring and win – I'd done it all. Where was I to go from there?

Things quietened down a bit once the fight was over, but I started missing the boxing. I carried on training, but for a while I didn't go anywhere near a boxing ring. I just did a lot of running. Then I just started thinking about doing it again – getting back in the ring. I couldn't resist it. So almost a year later in April 2003, after some serious training, I had another fight. This time against Lee Short. And we captured the spirit of the first fight all over again. The same electricity. The same magic. AND we raised a hell of a lot of money. Then in May I did it again, this time against Steve Miller.

Danny's Challenge, meanwhile, went from strength to strength. We raised £250,000 in eighteen months. It's not bad, is it? Loads of different people have benefited. £50,000 went to the Symbol Trust, which is a speech therapy group. Dan gets private speech therapy once a week and his speech is coming on tremendously. You can have a proper conversation with him. But if we weren't able to pay for him privately, his legal entitlement would be one hour's speech therapy per term – three hours a year. That's all these kids are entitled to from the government. We're lucky, we can afford extra. But there are a lot of kids out there whose parents can't afford it.

What if you're a single mum on a housing estate in Leeds, and you've got a kid with Down's Syndrome, and you can't afford to give him speech therapy? These kids need to communicate to get on in life. If they can't communicate people aren't going to talk to them and listen to them. If they can communicate, they're going to learn, and they're going to get a bit of respect, and they'll be able to get the things they need. So I think speech therapy is quite important.

What I envisaged was setting up these speech therapy groups for underprivileged kids and one day one of these kids would come up and thank me. It was like my big dream. Can you imagine that? This kid comes up and has a conversation, and you know it's because he had that speech therapy, which you played a part in providing.

But, speaking to Tessa Duffy from the Symbol Trust, she crushed the idea immediately. She said: "Do you know how many kids there are that need this? We're talking millions of pounds." We haven't got that sort of money, so I asked her what was the next best thing we could do to help with speech therapy. So she came back and said they'd been considering making videos for parents of children with learning disabilities to show them speech therapy techniques. She said they also wanted to make a video for teachers and carers too, to help them understand speech therapy, to enable them to put those techniques into practice in schools.

I loved the idea. They're brilliant these videos. The one for parents not only shows speech therapy techniques, it also shows these kids with Down's Syndrome at different stages in their lives doing different things. It's great because when you first find out your kid's got Down's Syndrome you're devastated and you don't know where to turn. You get given some poxy little book that tells you very little. This video shows kids reading, talking, playing, and it shows the speech therapy. Although it's hard to watch, it shows you that it ain't so bad. These kids are leading normal lives, and this is what they can expect to achieve. They needed £12,000 to produce the videos and £38,000 for distribution. A total of 20,000 videos were made with the help of Danny's Challenge.

We've also given £16,000 to an amazing woman called Alex Bell. At the Pride of Britain awards she was named the carer of the year. Alex is single, lives in Manchester, and has adopted nine children with Down's. I think she's mad. I've been round her house – it's a nuthouse. But it's lovely. It's on a hill just out-side Manchester, with a garden that goes right down behind the house. One of the children is blind, two are in wheel chairs. The more challenging the disability, it seems, the more Alex wants to take them on. She's an amazing character. She's got one room that's a play-room, which is all soft walls. The love in that house is phenomenal.

I'd read about her in the paper, and when we start-ed raising money, I thought – I want to help this woman. I remembered how hard I had found it to cope when we had Danny. Say Carol and I had been one of those couples who just couldn't cope with a child with

Down's and we'd put Dan up for adoption? I don't want to judge other people, but all children need a loving family. And this woman has made this wonderful loving family for children whose birth parents for whatever reason have been unable to. I thought: "I like this woman. I'm going to help her."

I managed to find out where she was so I rang up and told her who I was. I asked her if there was anything she needed. She said she had two kids who couldn't get down to the garden because of the steep incline, and they needed an electric lift. I drove up to Manchester to meet her. I went round her house and she showed me where she wanted it, so I got it and paid for it. It was £16,000 well spent.

Then we gave £15,000 to the Strathcona Theatre Company, which is made up of actors with learning disabilities. They put on these productions in front of junior doctors and it gives those doctors the chance to work with someone with a learning disability and to understand how to talk to them, which I thought was very important. In seven years of training, a junior doctor is exposed to people with learning disabilities for one day, which is unofficially known as "a visit to the funny farm". That needs changing.

Danny's Challenge has helped all sorts. We gave £150 to a church hall in Tunbridge Wells for a production some Down's kids were putting on, and flower arrangements. It just sounded nice what they were doing and they needed the money and I thought: "Yes, I'll pay for that."

I gave £2,500 to a young boy called Aaron Penn who had a learning disability but was also terminally ill. He wanted to go to Disneyland and Charlie Magri, the boxing guy, was trying to raise £5,000 for him. He'd raised £2,500 and they needed another £2,500. I gave them the money and this kid went to Florida. But I don't just hand out money; I get involved. I ring them up. I listen to them.

We gave £20,000 to the Outward Bound Trust, towards a project they're doing with children with learning disabilities. With the right training these kids can learn to abseil and go canoeing. You give us the money, it goes straight out again and these kids benefit directly. People can see where the money's going.

Everything was going brilliantly. I was really enjoying Danny's Challenge and the money was pouring in. I thought I'd do it for a year then give it up, but it wasn't like that. It just grew and grew. Sometimes I was so busy with it that wasn't able to get on with my work, but it was worth it. I've got a lot out of it. My profile grew. I did things I never would have done. I met people I never would have met. I even had lunch with Prince Andrew at Buckingham Palace! Can you believe it? I couldn't.

He wanted to meet me to discuss working with the Outward Bound Trust. When I drove through the gates of Buckingham Palace I sat in the back of my Bentley thinking: "This is bloody brilliant." I'm a kid from Ilford for God's sake. Twenty years ago I was selling string vests in Norfolk, and here I was living it up with the royals. I think you can make anything happen – well, I'm proof you can.

We were in that room where the royal family comes out onto the balcony. They told us not to look out because the tourists would get excited. It was great. I was walking down the corridor with Prince Andrew, having lunch in the Chinese room. And you think, who's sat in this room? And there I was, this boggy kid from the East End.

And another time we went to Downing Street for a reception for the Special Olympics committee. We were being introduced to Gordon Brown, Cherie Blair, Shirley Bassey. And it all came from Dan. None of it would have happened without him. Carol turned to me and said: "Aren't you glad we've got Dan?" I just think whatever happens to you, you can make something positive out of it.

When I had Dan, I just kept asking why? It shouldn't happen to me. It shouldn't happen to Danny Mardell. It should happen to Joe Bloggs round the corner, or that sad person down there. It doesn't happen to Danny Mardell, because I control things. Or I thought I did. And then it happened to me. It didn't feel right. I didn't want to know. I didn't want to know him. Frightening isn't it?

I've come a long way since then. I've learned a hell of a lot, about myself, about life. And little Dan? Well, he's just a great lad. He is quite amazing. I know I'm his parent, so I'm a bit biased, but he's a little bit different. He has got a special something about him. He just oozes love. Everywhere he goes he brings out the best in people. He doesn't always bring out the best in me – sometimes I lose my patience with him. He can be a bit demanding. He's a very early waker, and he won't go back to sleep and it's me he wants. Every morning I get up early to go to work and he's there, awake. Sometimes I leave home at 6.30am and he's up, he's with me. He's saying, "Don't go to work today, dad."

I don't know how long I can keep up the boxing. I'm 41 now. But it's been a fantastic opportunity for me. And I wouldn't have done any of it without little Dan. He's at the root of it all. Of everything. He's come such a long way. We all have. I've probably changed quite a bit as a person. I still drink, but not like I did. I'm really strict about my weight and keeping fit. My clothes have changed and I've probably become a lot more serious.

It probably caused problems in my marriage. Carol thinks I used to be fat and happy, then with Danny's Challenge I changed. The fights and everything meant

I didn't want to go out having a good time. It always used to be me wanting to go out of an evening and stay out. With Danny's Challenge and the boxing, that all changed, it was her wanting to stay out and have fun.

DANNY'S FUTURE

Someone once said to me that Danny's Challenge had reinvented me. I don't think it reinvented me. What it actually did was bring me back to where I had been years ago. It brought the old Danny Mardell back. For a long time I don't think I was being true to myself – all that living the high life and going to flash places. We spent a lot of money at that time. It was out of control.

I look back now and I think: "Jesus Christ, that was mad." We got through some serious wedge. It was a crazy lifestyle.

Soon after I started Danny's Challenge, in that short space of time, I think I got back to where I wanted to be in life. I was being myself again. I started liking myself again. I think Carol would say that I was always like myself – but from where I am now I think I was living a lie before then. Trying to be this person that wanted to be liked, wanted to be seen in all the right places. Now I don't really give a monkeys about all that and I'm back to the Danny Mardell I'm bloody happy with. And it was Danny's Challenge that brought that back.

When I was in serious training it was difficult for our relationship. I wasn't going out at all, because I didn't want to drink or eat too much so I just stayed in and Carol found her own niche of friends in Buckhurst Hill. I suppose we were growing apart a bit. We kept up the front very well, but our marriage was really in trouble.

Then, at a dealer conference in October 2002, there was a very attractive young girl. Far too young for me – she was only twenty-two or twenty-three – but I had an affair with her. I didn't see her that often, but I did have an affair. It was the first time in many, many years. It was the same time as Carol started this thing called the Friday Club which really gave me the hump. It was her and a bunch of friends meeting at an Italian restaurant in Woodford. Carol's such a flamboyant girl she draws people to her. She's got a fantastic character. So this club started and it got bigger and bigger and bigger. There were loads of guys in it and I started getting the right bloody hump. They'd go on from the restaurant to a nightclub in Buckhurst Hill. I didn't want to go down there because there was all this flashiness. I couldn't handle it.

We started to argue – a lot. It got to the point where it felt like we were constantly rowing, and on one occasion a television was thrown across the bloody kitchen. Dinner went one time. I walked out the house a couple of times. I came back a couple of times. I don't know what happened really. I suppose I went through some sort of mid-life crisis. I think Danny's Challenge made me have one, but I feel I'm out of it now. Finally I feel quite comfortable with myself.

The affair went on for quite some time. It was pretty sordid. We'd meet in hotels. The usual thing. Then on New Years Day 2003 Carol and I went up to

Langan's. We stayed in the West End and went out and got drunk together. We got on really well and she said to me, "I know you've had an affair. If you're willing to give it up now, whatever either of us have done in the past, let's draw a line in the sand and just move on." We shook hands and agreed that was it. I thought, fantastic. A week later I'm back with that girl again. Carol found out.

The last few years of our marriage, I think we were scared of splitting up. I think we both knew somewhere along the line we were going to go our separate ways. We couldn't carry on. By that time I don't think we were in love with each other. I wasn't the best husband. If I could have given Carol a hundred per cent devotion, then she'd be happy. But I can't do that, and she found that quite difficult, because she's a very beautiful girl, very funny, a fantastic character and I think she deserves someone who can devote themselves to her.

At the beginning we didn't spend a day apart. We were obsessed with each other – we didn't want to be out of each other's company, maybe because we didn't have that 100 per cent trust in each other. I think we're both people who knew quite easily we could find someone else, no problem at all.

But life changes with kids. I've been seeing a couple of girls recently – one in particular, but she wants to have kids one day and I can't do that. I don't ever want to have any more kids again. I'm glad I've got my kids and I wouldn't send them back. But I honestly believe they change your life dramatically. You don't get your life, you get their life. And twenty odd years of your life is wrapped around them, which is nice, but you tend to lose out on a lot of other things you could be doing.

I find that very difficult. You make this commitment to this young person and it's a hundred bloody per cent. It's there constantly. There's a lot of things in this life you can do, but with kids, you just can't. I know there are people who can be utterly selfless; who give up everything for their kids. I love my kids but I'm not like that. I'm not perfect. I am who I am.

After that New Year's Day, things didn't really get any better. I finished the affair, but Carol and I just weren't living together really. We were living in the same house. But we weren't together. She knew how desperately unhappy I was, I knew how unhappy she was. The kids were begging us to stop arguing and shouting at each other. It couldn't carry on. I couldn't live like that. So one weekend I walked out the house and spent it with my dad. I came back and had another argument.

I said I was going to leave, she said, "Why don't you just piss off?" I said: "I will." And I walked out and went and found a serviced flat in Docklands – seven hundred pounds a week it was. I moved into there. It was just before the Steve Miller fight in May 2003 and I thought, "I ain't going back."

Carol and I had six months of being at daggers with each other. We had solicitors' letters flying left right and centre. There were accusations all over the place. She's had a boyfriend I've bashed up. We had a roller coaster of a time. But after that, we seemed more able to make our peace.

I don't think the fact that Danny has Down's Syndrome made any difference. Our marriage problems had nothing to do with him, or the other two kids. But I suppose the thing with Danny that does feel different is that he's going to be there forever – he's going to have to be looked after for the rest of his life – and that makes everything even more difficult. I don't want Dan not to have a decent life. I don't want to let any of the kids down. It wasn't that I didn't want to live with them; I just couldn't live with their mother any more.

When it became clear the marriage was over and there was no going back, I moved out of the serviced flat and bought a place of my own in Docklands. Sometimes it feels absolutely fantastic. It's everything a man would dream of. You've got this single lifestyle, you've got a nice penthouse, you've got a nice few quid in your pocket, nice car, etc. But I've got to tell you, it isn't everything you think it is.

***

It's been a funny old time. I suppose Danny's Challenge opened my eyes a bit. I've met some very interesting people – from royalty down to East End villains and loads in-between. I can name quite a few top business people in the UK who are good mates of mine. A few people have said they'd like to work with me, and I was starting to feel a bit restless. I started thinking, what am I doing this for? Why am I working my nuts off selling copiers, when I can quite easily walk into an office, do a deal with somebody, and walk out with lots of money. Very easily. I've done it. I thought to myself, I've got all these bloody talents that I'm not using, so I decided to start using them. I wanted a completely different way of working.

So I sold the business. I was offered a few quid for it. It got rid of a nice few debts, left me with a nice bit of money in my pocket, and it enabled me to do a couple of things I've wanted to. I've made investments in a couple of other businesses. I've taken a percentage of a futures company.

Things are happening in my life. Barbara Cassani from the London Olympic bid team contacted me recently. She'd read about me in the *Times* and invited me up to the fiftieth floor of Canary Wharf to have a meeting with them about working with them on the 2012 project. They said they could parachute in any celebrity to represent them for the Olympics, but they wanted a man on the ground. A businessman from Stratford who could go out and talk on their behalf.

So they asked me to join them and I said yes, for obvious reasons.

So it's all change. End of marriage, end of business, it's a new life. And do you know what the most exciting thing is? I don't know what I'm going to do, but I know I'm going to do something. I've got a rough idea – I'll be using my contacts to help people to build their businesses, networking people together, taking percentages of their businesses, being the man that fixes things, gets things done.

The best thing about it all is that Carol and I can go out together now and have a good time. We had lunch out together for my birthday the other day. She's such a glamorous girl. Do you know what I miss? I forget how good-looking she is. I walked into this restaurant with her, and there were all these guys staring at her – and I thought, I haven't seen this for a few months. Everyone was looking at her. She's stunning. I'd forgotten about that. If she's had affairs I can't blame her. I've done the same. I hope she finds someone, but let's hope he's a proper geezer. Not a shirker.

The kids have kind of accepted that I don't live with them any more. They see me at least twice, maybe three times a week. They come over and stay, or I go and take them out. At the beginning it was quite difficult, but now I've got my flat and it's all sorted it's fine. In fact, I spend more quality time with them now than when I was at home. I'm actually doing a lot more with them.

Take one typical weekend. In the evening I took them to *Chitty Chitty Bang Bang*; we left there and went to Hamley's; then we went to a restaurant. We got home to my flat about 10.30pm, then next morning we got up, went to the pictures, went to the park. Then we went home to their house. Carol joined us and we all went to the circus together. Jesus Christ they're wearing me out!

I can't say they're happy I've moved out. They want me there. They've said: "Why don't you want to live at home, dad?" And I've said: "Look, me and your mum can't get on at the moment." And they've kind of accepted that. They've got used to it now. They're lovely kids. Little Danny's OK. He hasn't said a lot about it. He's sort of got on with it. It seems to have affected Pia more than either Frank or Dan.

It has also presented some difficulties with Danny's

Challenge, keeping up a front of a happy family. Don't get me wrong, I'd do anything for my kids and I'm really proud of what I've done with Danny's Challenge. It's been really exciting, but now I look back at it, the problems in our relationship have made me feel a fraud.

We were doing all this stuff – me and Carol were parading around like this perfect glamorous couple, playing happy families with Prince Andrew and all that. But in fact our marriage was coming apart at the seams. It was difficult living a lie, trying to look like the perfect family. When the one documentary team turned up one morning – they were featuring me in their programme *Fitness Files* – they arrived and Carol and me had just had the most horrendous punch-up. Not physical, but it was awful. And there she was telling the cameras a few minutes later what a wonderful father I am, what a great husband I am. Whenever I watch that documentary I think if only people knew what was going on an hour beforehand!

We were in the limelight to such an extent, that I couldn't really tell anyone what was happening. I was scared shitless. I didn't know what to do. I wanted to leave home, but I was worried about the kids, and I was worried about Danny's Challenge. I confided in a couple of friends and they both told me in different ways that I couldn't carry on living a lie if I wasn't happy there. "It's your life as well," they said. "You've got to get on with it." My mates told me: "Danny, you're loving your kids, you're looking after your kids, it's just you're not getting on with your wife. It happens to people every day, why should you be any different? People accept it. They just get on with their lives, they won't think any less of you."

And that's what's happened. The truth is, I'm not the perfect family man, it's not me. I'm a good dad. I love my kids. But I don't think I'm a particularly good husband. Does that make sense? In fact the reaction I've had has been fine. I was expecting some serious problems out of this, but it hasn't happened.

I'm never ever going to get married again. I'll guarantee you that, never ever again. I prefer having a girlfriend to a wife. If it's easy to leave then I think you work harder. As soon as you have a ring on your finger, you start taking the other person for granted, and the love goes out the bloody window and I don't like that. I'm quite a romantic bloke. I do like love and all the business that goes with it. But marriage? I've done it twice and, much as I loved Carol, I'm not doing it again.

**

Danny's Challenge carries on despite the changes in my life. I'm still committed to it – 100 per cent – but these days I'm more worried about how people will perceive me. It scares me. I'm campaigning as this father – who's come on this amazing journey with his Down's Syndrome son – but I don't even live with him. So why am I doing it?

I worry that people will think I'm doing it for me, to raise my profile, but I'm not. What matters to me is raising awareness about people with learning disabilities. I want to carry it on, but I do worry about people's perception of me. I was seen as the fantastic family man, but then I walked out and left my kids.

In the end I have to think we've done the best thing for the kids by splitting up – including Danny. It was awful for them seeing me and Carol argue and fight like that. They're a lot happier now. Pia misses me something awful. It's a daughter-dad thing. She's completely besotted with me.

When it's Pia's birthday, I always take her to a good restaurant. When she was two, I took her to and had her birthday party there, and I got the chef to sign the menu. When she was three, I took her to the Dorchester; when she was four I took her to the Windows of the World at the top of the Hilton, and when she was five I took her to the Ivy. I always walk out with the menu and get it signed by the chef. They've all been framed and they hang around her bedroom wall, so when she's eighteen years old she can look at all these different menus and know she's been to all the great restaurants in London on her birthday with her dad. And when that spotty teenager turns up with that bloody Mark 3 Cortina and wants to take her down to Pizza Hut, she'll tell him to piss off!

But I do have my worries. Sometimes I've started to think I am a bad father because I've left Danny and the other two. But everyone who sees the kids around me – and the way we are together – says they think I'm a good father. I see them every other weekend, when they stay with me. Then during the week I will have one of them individually, so I get special time with each of them.

With Dan we normally go and have a bit of Chinese. He loves Chinese. We go to a restaurant which is right by City Airport and watch the planes come into land. He'll eat a big plate of noodles – he's noodles mad. The trouble with Dan is he doesn't know when to stop eating – he will eat until he's sick so you have to watch him.

Always with Dan, we have to ring my mum up in Spain so he has a chat with her. They've got this special thing, my mum and Dan – he went to stay with her in the summer. He's picked up a few words in Spanish, he has made some little friends out there.

Dan loves his mum. I know he cries for me quite a lot; when he is with me, he cries for his mum. I feel bad because I'm not there to protect him. I've got worries about the future, but I think I would know if something was wrong – the other two would tell me. They are quite open kids and they do tell me things. I'm seriously worried about the bullying side. Not just because of what I was like, but because I know what kids are like. When they're thirteen, fourteen, fifteen, they don't want to be talking to the kid with his tongue hanging out. It's not cool to be talking to someone who is different.

Dan's already got a girlfriend, though. He had one girlfriend – he dumped her. He said: " I don't love her any more." He loves this girl Sophie now. He brought her a bracelet in Spain. "I'm going to marry Sophie Shepherd and I'm always kissing Sophie Shepherd."

I hope he does have a relationship when he grows up. But what happens if he does fall in love with some girl from school? The girl might be just being nice to him. He'd get hurt. It would be easier to explain to Frankie if a girl dumps him. But Danny's going to be a teenager soon. He'll need a lot of things explaining to him. He is a Mr Love. Everything is love with Danny. There isn't much nastiness in Dan.

I changed my Will the other day. With Dan I need to make sure that all his needs are catered for all his life. It will need a little bit of explaining to my other two. A lot more will go to Dan than to them two, so he can be looked after forever if I'm not around. When I was doing this Will, they were asking me: "What if Danny has children?" I said: "I haven't really thought about that." If Danny did have children and he had a Down's Syndrome wife, for example, the chance of him having a Down's Syndrome child is quite high. We've got to think about what happens there. Financially, Danny's fine for the rest of his life, but the other stuff I can't be sure about.

The other two are very good with him. He plays with the pair of them. Frankie and Dan have got a great friendship. They play a lot together. There isn't a lot Danny can't do and they're good together the two brothers. Pia is starting to show she is a very helpful, loving little girl. If Danny can't open his ice lolly, she will help him. If Danny needs help, she's there for him. I don't know what's going to happen in the future. I can imagine her being the big sister to him. She will want to have her own life, but I think she will be looking out for him.

***

I tell you what was nice. The kids were with me one

weekend. I took my three, plus two of their mates to Digger Land in Kent. It was a great day. I drove them home and, as soon as we got back, they all jumped out and they all went running to the conker tree down the road to get conkers.

It's a cul-de-sac and a private road where they live and there isn't much traffic. They ran and they all knew exactly where they were going, including little Dan. It all felt so safe and so nice. I drove away that day thinking – I'm glad they're where they are, that they're in the house they want to be in. Dan's happy now, and, despite all the crap that's been going on between me and Carol, the kids' environment hasn't changed that much. Carol and me might be over, but it ain't the end of the world.

I'm proud of my kids. They're great kids. All of them. They're getting a fantastic education – they're learning the piano, they're speaking French and playing the guitar. All the things I've never done. And Danny's doing fantastic. His speech is brilliant. I'm so proud of the progress he's made.

And I'm as committed to Danny's Challenge as I ever was. At the time of writing this, we have raised

£300,000 in total. Plans for another fight are under way and I've gone back into training. I'm also planning to climb Everest in 2005. I can't miss an opportunity like that. How fantastic! Imagine it. You're on your deathbed, you've got your kids round you and your grandkids:

"What have you done in your life granddad?"

"I've climbed Everest!"

No matter how successful you've been in the rest of your life, no matter what you've done, you've been 29,000 feet up Everest. You can't argue with that. AND I could get a million quid out of it for charity!

I've done very well out of Danny's Challenge. Of course I have. But that's not the point. I still feel passionately about campaigning to raise awareness about Down's Syndrome and learning difficulties. Particularly when I read in my newspaper that they're considering screening all pregnant women for Down's Syndrome.

They treat people with Down's like second-class citizens. If a Down's child needs an operation, the NHS won't do it because they think their quality of life is not the same. If they go ahead and screen all women, it's like creating a master race. "If you're not perfect we're going to abort you." The reason they want to abort you is because the cost of looking after someone with Down's Syndrome is a lot higher than somebody without it. The chances are they might have a hole in the heart, or a kidney problem, eyesight problems, whatever it might be, so therefore they think it will put more of a strain on the NHS.

If people do want to be screened and they find they've got a child with Down's, and they make the decision to have a termination, that's fine. It's up to them. But I fear the NHS will offer screening to all women – not to be caring towards potential parents, but to discourage couples from having a child with Down's because of the cost long-term to the NHS. It's bloody cynical.

I read a piece in the *Daily Mail* the other day by a woman who had aborted her child who had Down's. The way she was talking, it was like she'd done everybody a favour – like she'd done the child a favour. It was like she was a bloody saint. I know some people can't handle it. If we'd found out Danny was Down's Syndrome, we would have probably aborted him. We know that, me and Carol. But the way that woman wrote that article, she couldn't ever have met anyone with Down's. I don't blame her for the abortion. I really don't. I don't have a problem with that at all. But she shouldn't write that she was doing that child a favour. She wasn't.

People with Down's can lead rich, fulfilled and absolutely fantastic lives. There's one woman I know, an artist, who lives with her boyfriend who has a learning disability. They're leading the most fantastic life. They're looking after each other and they're talking about having a family. And why shouldn't they? People with Down's do have children, though it's very rare.

When me and Carol were together in Chingford, I always had it in my mind that if the house next door came up for sale I'd buy it, with the sole aim that if when Danny is older he wants a house, he could live next door to us. That was my plan. Now we're not together, Carol might have a different agenda altogether. But if he wanted a place I'd buy him one.

I'm taking it as it comes. I hope one day he will lead a semi-independent life. A lot of Down's kids live in sheltered accommodation – living on their own but with a helper that comes in. There might be three or four people living together in a house with a carer either in the house or very close by. I like that idea. I'd like him to have a job. He loves animals. I can see him living on a farm. Perhaps I can make that happen for him, if he wanted that. And that would be lovely.

Of course, like any parent, I'm worried what will happen when we're not around. People with Down's live into their seventiess now, so he's very likely to outlive us. I hope he does but I do worry who will look after him when we are not around. Will Frankie and Pia look after him? Will they be the kind of people to look after their brother? I don't know. I try not to think about it.

***

Danny is starting to understand he has got Down's Syndrome. He says: "I've got Down's Syndrome. Why have I got Down's Syndrome?" I just say: "I don't know Dan. It just happened to you. He understands that he's different, that he's got something. He is surrounded by people who don't take a blind bit of notice, but he knows it now.

I think he's going to have a tough few years with other kids. It does worry me that I'm not really there to look out for him. I was thinking the other day how nice it would be to be sleeping with my kids, in the same house. Not just Dan, all of them. In some ways, people say I've got the best of all worlds – a good living, great kids, but not all the time. It's the day to day thing with the kids I miss. Carol would never stop me seeing them, but I can only see them in those allocated times. It's not the same, is it? But I'm not into all that Fathers 4 Justice thing. The last thing I want to do is dress up as Batman. Who's going to sympathise with that?

Having a child with learning disabilities, you hear these people saying: "I've been blessed." What a load of bollocks. You've got to look after this person for the rest of your life. You're not blessed, you've got yourself a bit of a problem. But now Dan's here and the love you get from a boy like Danny is amazing. We'll just make sure he gets what he needs.

**

I don't know where I'm going to be in five years time. Maybe I will set up in Spain, near my mum. Would I want little Dan living with me permanently – just me and him? Probably not. I would probably find that very, very difficult. With Danny – well, maybe he won't want to go and have this independent life on his own. In a few years time when I've settled down a bit more, I might like it. He's a good guy. He's a nice character – people like him.

Last week we went to one of those indoor play centres in Epping. Frankie ran off with his mate, then Danny ran off and I couldn't see him anywhere at all. I looked everywhere – you know what those places are like – and there he was, running around with this other boy about the same age. He'd made a bond with this kid – and they were climbing all over the place. And I watched this, and I felt this huge pride. We'd come to this place and, completely on his own, he'd made a friend. That boy had accepted Dan, just the way he is – and that was a good feeling. Dan does that quite a lot – he makes friends very easily. It's quite a gift.

But then, the other day, I took the kids to McDonald's. I'm up buying the meals when all of a sudden Frankie has come up to me. "Dad, them boys over there just called Danny fucking stupid," he says. There were four or five of these boys, aged about thirteen or fourteen. I just saw red. There was this one and I went up to him. I don't know exactly what's been said, so I said: "Did you just swear at my son?"

Pia said: "He called him a wanker, dad."

I said "What?"

Dan said: "He did."

I said to him: "Did you just say that to my son? Listen here. If you say anything to my son, I'm coming back for you. You leave him alone. You eat your dinner and leave my kids alone." It's the first time I've had to do that. I felt so wild. I couldn't really eat my dinner properly after that. The great thing about it was the way the three of them stuck together.

There was another time, last year, when it snowed quite badly. We went to this bistro in Chingford. As we've gone in there's these kids throwing snowballs at people. These are not nice kids, you know the sort – they're throwing these snowballs at everyone and anyone, not particularly Dan, but Dan's crying his eyes out. He's trying to get in, and I've run out at these kids. They're teenagers, six or seven of them. I'm slipping all over the place and I'm thinking, I'm going to bloody ring their necks. Dan's crying his eyes out. Frankie's saying, "Dad, let's go and get them. I know how to do an upper cut. Let's go and bash them." It was quite funny. But Dan felt he was being singled out. He wasn't, but he thought he was. He said: "Why were they throwing them at me?" But it wasn't just him, it was anyone. He still talks about those snowballs to this day. He didn't like it at all.

It's like when he first went to school. This kid made him eat flowers. He doesn't like flowers now. The head teacher dealt with it very well and nipped it in the bud (so to speak), but Dan still can't go near flowers and that was years ago. If we go into a restaurant and there are flowers on the table, we have to move them. Pia moves them. He can't stand flowers around him.

***

196

As I write this, my divorce is about to come through. In an ideal world I would still be living with little Danny and the other kids. But I'll always be their dad and I'm a good dad. It took me a while to get there, god knows, but I do believe I've become a better person as a result of Danny. I'm still a selfish bastard. I don't think I can change that, but I do treat people a little differently now, especially underprivileged people.

If I see someone selling the *Big Issue*, I'll always buy a copy. Before, I would have thought: "You lazy bastard, go and get a job." I won't give money to beggars, but I will buy them a cup of tea or a meal. I wouldn't have done that years ago. I used to have this attitude that anyone can do what I've done; anyone can make money and make a success of their lives. I used to think we were all can-dos, it was just that some people couldn't be bothered to. But over the last few years I've come to the view that there aren't that many can-dos out there. We're not all like that. We all have different abilities.

It's been a long time coming but I think I've learned to respect others for what they are. I realise we all have a different place in life. The whole experience of Danny and what followed has brought me down a peg or two. I understand now that we all do what we can.

When you meet someone like Alex Bell, a single woman who has adopted nine children with Down's Syndrome, you think, "How can I be a better person than her?" She's lucky if she gets four hours' sleep a night. If I'd met her a few years ago, I would've thought: "You silly cow." I was always suspicious of "do-gooders". I couldn't understand what they were after. But I've changed. I now go out of my way to talk to people with learning difficulties. I believe they should be accepted as equals and I think they should be given every opportunity to reach their full potential. They've got the same rights as anyone else. They shouldn't be refused operations like second-class citizens.

This process of change in me hasn't happened over night. It's taken a long, long time. It's been an extraordinary journey. I've changed as a family man and as a businessman too. I'm still a bit of a wheeler dealer, but I've grown up a lot. As you get older you slow down. Whether Dan has made me mature, I don't know.

Maybe. Maybe I would have grown up anyway. But the last three years, I've calmed right down.

I think Dan has made me confront things I would never have confronted if I hadn't had him. He has made me a more tolerant person. I'm not perfect, far from it. Just ask Carol. But I'm better than I was. A lot better. And who have I got to thank for that? Little Danny.

Thanks, Dan. Thank you, my son.

If you would like further information or support regarding Down's syndrome please contact:

The Down's Syndrome Association

For all enquiries including referral to local support groups, information, fundraising & membership.

Langdon Down Centre
2a Langdon Park
Teddington
TW11 9PS

Tel: 0845 230 0372
Fax: 0845 230 0373
Email: info@downs-syndrome.org.uk

I'm A Teacher
Get Me Out of Here!
Francis Gilbert
1-904095-68-2

At last, here it is. The book that tells you the unvarnished truth about teaching. By turns hilarious, sobering, and downright horrifying, *I'm a Teacher, Get me Out of Here* contains the sort of information that you won't find in any school prospectus, government advert, or Hollywood film.

In this astonishing memoir, Francis Gilbert candidly describes the remarkable way in which he was trained to be a teacher, his terrifying first lesson and his even more frightening experiences in his first job at Truss comprehensive, one of the worst schools in the country.

Follow Gilbert on his rollercoaster journey through the world that is the English education system; encounter thuggish and charming children, terrible and brilliant teachers; learn about the sinister effects of school inspectors and the teacher's disease of 'controloholism'. Spy on what really goes on behind the closed doors of inner-city schools.

"Gilbert is a natural storyteller. I read this in one jaw-dropping gulp."
Tim Brighouse, Commissioner for London Schools, TES

My Brief Career
The trials of a young lawyer
Harry Mount
1-904095-69-0

My Brief Career, Harry Mount's hilarious account of his hellish year as a "pupil" – a trainee barrister in The Temple – has all the horror of a Dickensian tragedy and all the charm of Bridget Jones' Diaries. An exposé of what goes on behind the ancient walls of London's inns of court, this fascinating story dares to reveal the grim secrets of one of England's most archaic institutions. This is a book for everyone who has ever thought they might want to become a lawyer.

"A horribly funny study of boredom, vanity and folly"
Daily Telegraph

"A hilarious account of the splendid miseries of being a pupil in a barrister's chambers"
John Mortimer

How to be a Bad Birdwatcher
To the greater glory of life
Simon Barnes
1-904095-95-X

Look out of the window.
See a bird.
Enjoy it.
Congratulations. You are now a bad birdwatcher.

Anyone who has ever gazed up at the sky or stared out of the window knows something about birds. In this funny, inspiring, eye-opening book, Simon Barnes paints a riveting picture of how bird-watching has framed his life and can help us all to a better understanding of our place on this planet.

How to be a bad birdwatcher shows why birdwatching is not the preserve of twitchers, but one of the simplest, cheapest and most rewarding pastimes around.

"An ode to the wild world outside the kitchen window"
Daily Telegraph

The Cruel Mother
A Family Ghost Laid to Rest
Siân Busby
1-904095-71-2

In 1919 Siân Busby's great-grandmother, Beth, gave birth to triplets. One of the babies died at birth and eleven days later Beth drowned the surviving twins in a bath of cold water. She was sentenced to an indefinite term of imprisonment at Broadmoor.

The murder and the deep sense of shame it generated obviously affected Beth, her husband and their surviving children to an extraordinary degree, but it also resounded through the lives of her grandchildren and great-grandchildren.

In Siân's case, ill-suppressed knowledge of the event manifested itself in recurring nightmares and contributed towards a prolonged bout of post-natal depression. After the birth of her second son, she decided to investigate the story once and for all and lay to rest the ghosts which have haunted the family for 80 years…

"A gripping tale of madnss and infanticide during the Great War... Powerful and disturbing"
Margaret Forster

The Irresistible Con (paperback)
The bizarre life of a fraudulent genius
Francis Wheen
1-904095-74-7

His names were crazy enough – Baron Hajdu, Carl Rodgers, Mr Carl, Michael Karoly. And his jobs – receptionist, hypnotherapist, businessman, rentier, journalist and sex worker... But he was always careful to cover his tracks, so noone suspected a thing when in 1971 a curious new figure appeared on the London academic scene.

Her name was Charlotte Bach, and she was a broad-shouldered mammoth of a woman, with a deep voice and a heavy Central European accent. She was a former lecturer at the University of Budapest, and had a new theory of sex and evolution which was soon being heralded as one of the greatest intellectual advances of the 20th century...

The Irresistible Con is the gloriously bizarre story of a conman extraordinaire, and one of Francis Wheen's funniest pieces of writing yet.

"An extraordinary tale"
Mail on Sunday

Camilla (paperback)
An Intimate Portrait
Rebecca Tyrrel
1-904095-73-9

In this gripping portrait, Rebecca Tyrrel paints a vivid picture of the life of Camilla Parker Bowles – jolly, horsey, laid-back Camilla, loyal friend, loving mother, whose 'open' county marriage was none of anyone's business until it emerged that the other man in it was the heir to the throne...

To her critics, Camilla will always be a destructive marriage-breaker, the woman who took on the People's Princess and won. But, if nothing else, she is constant – a dignified consort, who has endured years of public vilification and never answered back.

With the help of friends and county contacts, royal reporters and palace insiders, Tyrrel goes behind the scenes of an extraordinary love story – a scandalous tale of romance and tragedy, which has rocked the monarchy to its foundations and yet doggedly prevailed. Welcome to Camilla's world..

"Very funny... blissfully gossipy" India Knight

"Juicy, deliciously naughty and revelatory"
Sunday Independent

In case of difficulty in purchasing any Short Books
title through normal channels, please contact
BOOKPOST Tel: 01624 836000
Fax: 01624 837033
email: bookshop@enterprise.net
www.bookpost.co.uk
Please quote ref. 'Short Books'